"An insightful, sobering yet ultimately empowering book. The depth of the research is extremely impressive, the arguments clear and persuasive. A must-read for anyone interested in the future of the planet."
Charlotte Uhlenbroek, biologist, writer and TV presenter

"A great manual on how to get the planning and action for dealing with climate change right – borrowing partly from the principles of successful transformation processes in organizations. But does the capacity to do it exist? This is the worrying question we are left to contemplate."
Vicky Pryce, former Joint Head, Government Economic Service

"This is a groundbreaking book! To address the urgency of climate change the book challenges us to address the social and economic issues of our civilization as well. The technological solutions can only go so far; we need to go further and need to embrace a new paradigm. This book gives readers a most comprehensive understanding of climate problems as well as climate solutions."
Satish Kumar, Founder, Schumacher College

"As a passionate ~~~ ul analysis reinforces the w lanet, and challenges us al equired." Jonathan A ctic Infrastru e,

_____ Survey

"Revelatory! Richard unwinds the complexity in the perils of continuing our free-market economic models to deliver timely prescriptives for an environmentally sustainable, socially equitable and achievable economic recovery."
Amos White, Vice-Chair of the Climate Emergency Mobilization Task Force (USA), Founder and Chief Planting Officer of 100K Trees for Humanity

"Richard has produced an evidenced and detailed consideration of our difficulties and state of inertia, but is optimistic and sets out how we can transform our lives. He puts climate change and the avoidance of global warming at the centre and calls for a new commitment for our sustainability. This book is a crucial part of this commitment."
Jeff Gold, Professor of Organisation Learning at Leeds and York Business Schools

"Richard Joy dares to face reality and surprises with advantageous outcomes of refraining from economic growth. An inspiring, versatile master reflection on sociopolitical systems for realists and doers!"
Kirsten M. Florentine Weber, Climate Physicist at the Grantham Centre for Sustainable Futures, University of Sheffield and Co-Chair of the Environmental Sustainability Rotary Action Group (ESRAG), Great Britain & Ireland

UNSUSTAINABLE

The Urgent Need to Transform Society and Reverse Climate Change

Richard Joy

BRISTOL
UNIVERSITY
PRESS

First published in Great Britain in 2021 by

Bristol University Press
University of Bristol
1-9 Old Park Hill
Bristol
BS2 8BB
UK
t: +44 (0)117 954 5940
e: bup-info@bristol.ac.uk

Details of international sales and distribution partners are available at
bristoluniversitypress.co.uk

© Bristol University Press 2021–2026

British Library Cataloguing in Publication Data
A catalogue record for this book is available from the British Library

ISBN 978-1-5292-1802-2 paperback
ISBN 978-1-5292-1803-9 ePub
ISBN 978-1-5292-1804-6 ePdf

The right of Richard Joy to be identified as author of this work has been asserted by
him in accordance with the Copyright, Designs and Patents Act 1988.

Cover design: Clifford Hayes
Front cover image: Getty Images/Ted Mead
Bristol University Press uses environmentally responsible print partners.
Printed and bound in Great Britain by CMP, Poole

Contents

List of Figures and Tables

Figures

Tables

Preface

It is increasingly clear that climate change threatens the future of the planet. Immediate and radical action is required, yet the current pace of change seems unlikely to provide an effective response. This book seeks to understand the reasons for this lack of action and it considers whether our political and economic institutions are capable of managing the rapid scale of transformation that is required.

The idea for this book resulted from numerous discussions with my father, an academic who taught at the University of Cambridge, London School of Economics and as a professor at University of Sussex. He also has many years' consulting experience with United Nations (UN) agencies. Over the last few years, we have become increasingly concerned that the current socio-economic model is unsustainable and this book brings together his experience as an academic, and my own perspective as a consultant specializing in strategic change.

This book is not a rant at big business or politicians – well, maybe in parts – nor is it a message of gloom and hopelessness. Instead, it seeks to understand the reasons why there has been such a lack of action when it is clear that the current trajectory is heading for disaster. As well as examining the causes of this apparent inertia, the book seeks to identify the drivers of change that could help us move towards a more sustainable socio-economic model.

The book also expresses frustration with intergovernmental organizations, governments and politicians. However, any criticisms need to be balanced with an acknowledgement that many governments and politicians do recognize the need to act and many of them, including the UK government, are starting to place the environment high on their political agenda.

The term *vested interests* is used rather frequently and it is probably worth clarifying that this is a shorthand for organizations and individuals that use their wealth, power and influence to protect activities that would be disrupted by requirements to operate more sustainably. In simple terms, profits would be reduced if organizations had to account for the environmental cost of their activities. However, this frequent reference to the apparently dark and sinister forces of *vested interests* is not a blanket condemnation of all corporate organizations. There are many organizations doing amazing things to speed the transition to a sustainable society and this book is rooted in the idea that the drive towards a more sustainable society needs to be led by innovative business leaders and must utilize the strengths of the market economy. Many organizations already see the commercial imperative to operate more sustainably and recognize the financial and reputational benefits that this brings. There is a growing number of business leaders who are transforming their organizations by their conviction, morality and vision. Their ability to drive change is one of the primary sources of hope that a sustainable future is within our grasp. This determination to build a more sustainable society is also reflected in many small businesses that are finding new ways to save our environment and serve their communities.

There is no doubt that the planet is on a dangerous trajectory, but this book believes that radical social, economic and political change is possible. Indeed, it is not only possible but the process of transition offers huge potential benefits and should be seen as an opportunity for civilization to evolve for the better. While acknowledging that some positive change is already happening, this book is critical of the pace of change and the collective failure of the international community to commit to actions that will achieve the necessary reduction in greenhouse gas emissions within the very limited period that is available.

To understand the scale of the challenge that we face it is useful to reference a statement by Sir David Attenborough at the 2018 Climate Change Conference held in Katowice, Poland. His address to the conference warned of the urgent need for leaders to take action. "Right now, we are facing a man-made disaster of global scale. Our greatest threat in thousands of years.

Climate Change. If we don't take action the collapse of our civilizations and the extinction of much of the natural world is on the horizon."

Reversing the current trajectory of global warming will require unprecedented levels of international cooperation, both politically and across the corporate world. However, it is not only political and corporate change that is required, there also needs to be a transformation in the values, attitudes and beliefs that underpin our societies and economic systems.

This book will frequently refer to *climate change* but this should be interpreted broadly as encompassing all the various facets of climate change and global warming. In addition, climate change should also be recognized as intricately linked to changes within the natural environment. Not only does damage to the environment affect the climate, such as the destruction of rain forest, but climate change has a dramatic impact on all aspects of life on earth. The interdependency between the climate and the natural environment creates a complex system where rising global temperatures trigger events that cause feedback loops, which in turn amplify the causes of climate change. The nightmare scenario is that we reach a tipping point and the feedback effects trigger runaway global warming, and human intervention becomes powerless to reverse ever-increasing global temperatures.

This book is offered in the hope that it might influence opinion and support informed discussion. It offers ideas and proposals, but it is cautious of offering *solutions*, as the scale of the problem is so vast and the complexity of detail so overwhelming that it is impossible to give a definitive answer. Instead, the focus is more on clarifying the principles that need to be understood, identifying the capabilities required and defining the factors that influence outcomes.

At its heart, this book seeks to address the question: *Is our current civilization likely to survive?* To answer this question it considers the scale of the challenge we face, the potential consequences if we fail to address it and most significantly, if we possess the capabilities that are required to manage a process of radical social and economic change.

During the period of writing this book (about five years), the scientific projections were continually changing. At the start, there was a broad sense that climate change was serious but manageable. Over the next few years, there was a growing sense that the world was heading for an environmental disaster and that we are perilously close to the tipping point. Hopefully, we have not yet reached that point, but it is increasingly clear that human civilization is in real and imminent danger. Unless the causes of global warming are addressed immediately, there is a very real possibility that we may pass the tipping point, leading to runaway global warming.

The structure of the book

This book is in three parts:

- Part I considers the current state of the world and the need for sustainable social and economic development.
- Part II addresses the process of change and the capabilities required if we are to transition to a sustainable socio-economic model.
- Part III considers the practical actions that each of us can take.

A recurring theme throughout the book is the idea that significant change will only happen when political leaders are subject to scrutiny from an informed electorate and corporate leaders respond to the demands of environmentally conscious consumers. Hopefully, this book will raise awareness of the problems we face, enable the actions of politicians to be evaluated and encourage consumers to support those organizations that demonstrate environmental accountability.

PART 1

The State of the World

Part I provides a review of the key scientific data relating to the causes of climate change and sets out the implications of this scientific evidence.

There is overwhelming agreement within the scientific community that climate change is real, happening fast and threatening the future of the natural environment that supports life on earth. The difficulty facing anyone in reviewing the scientific evidence is that it is not always easy to find a single, definitive answer. There is a massive volume of data from a multitude of sources. Researchers are continually publishing reports and our understanding of the data is always evolving. During the course of writing this book it quickly became apparent that the more we learnt, the more we understood about the extent of the dangers that we faced. Each new revelation suggested that things were worse than we had previously thought.

1

Setting the Context

Chapter summary

This chapter offers an initial assessment of the key scientific data, including a brief explanation of how global temperatures are measured and two of the key indicators used to track carbon in the atmosphere. This chapter also considers the rate of reduction that will be required if global emissions of greenhouse gases are to be limited to levels that will avoid a rise greater than 1.5°C. There is a brief explanation of the difference between economic growth, development and sustainability, as the ability to distinguish these three terms has important implications for policy decisions by governments. Finally, the chapter raises the need for a new economic model, rather than perpetuating the current industrial economic model that is dependent on mass consumerism, the exploitation of the natural world and a failure to account for the environmental, economic and social consequences that inevitably follow.

The basic problem

Human activity is consuming the world's resources at a rate that cannot be supported. In addition, our industrialized economies are damaging the atmosphere, the oceans and the natural world with drastic consequences for the delicate balance of the planet's natural equilibrium. It is clear that climate change is happening and that human activity is pushing us along a trajectory that may soon become irreversible.

Although CO_2 is the primary cause of human related global warming, other greenhouse gases include methane, in large part from animal agriculture, nitrous oxide, much of it caused by agricultural fertilizers, and a multitude of industrially produced gases, particularly refrigerants. The scientific evidence is unambiguous and the emission of greenhouse gases has to be virtually eliminated.

Much of the debate on greenhouse gases focuses on CO_2, and climate scientists will often refer to *parts per million* or the *carbon budget*, where:

- Parts per million measures a given concentration of CO_2, and this is linked to a projected increase in global temperatures.
- Carbon budget is an estimate of the maximum limit on the total cumulative number of tonnes of CO_2 that can be released into the atmosphere for any given rise in global temperatures.

These values are estimated, but information produced by the Intergovernmental Panel on Climate Change (IPCC) has the following projections.

Parts per million

Parts per million, as at March 2021 was 417.64 ppm. This represents an increase of 2.9 ppm compared to levels 12 months previously.[1] Predicting the future rate of carbon emissions is difficult since there the demand for energy is increasing and the rate of conversion to zero emission energy is uncertain. A quote from an IPCC report emphasizes the urgent need to halt the use of fossil fuels.

> Despite extraordinary growth in renewable fuels over the past decade, the global energy system is still dominated by fossil fuel sources. The annual increase in global energy use is greater than the increase in renewable energy, meaning that fossil fuel use continues to grow. This growth needs to halt immediately. (IPCC Report. Landmark United in Science Report Informs Climate Action Summit, September 2019)

Carbon budget

The carbon budget is used to calculate the relationship between rises in global temperatures and carbon emissions. Based on projections of the rate at which CO_2 is emitted into the atmosphere this data seeks to estimate how many years it will take to reach a given rise in global temperature. The scientific projections vary. Some forecasts suggest that the 1.5°C threshold may be reached in 15–20 years. Other forecasts suggest that the existing atmospheric carbon emissions are already at levels that will take us past the 1.5°C threshold. Even an optimistic interpretation of the data shows that we only have a few years left in which to become net-zero.

Carbon emissions remain in the atmosphere for decades. It takes up to 200 years for 80 per cent of CO_2 emissions to be absorbed by the oceans, although this increases the concentration of CO_2 in the oceans causing another set of problems. It takes hundreds of years for carbon emissions to be completely absorbed by natural processes, so even if we stopped emitting CO_2 immediately, we would be living with the consequences for several hundred years.

Average global temperatures

It is important to understand what is being measured when there is discussion of *average global temperatures*. At first sight, it might seem almost irrelevant to worry about a 1°C increase in global temperature, since we know that temperatures continually change with the seasons and that the range of temperatures in different parts of the world can vary enormously. Also, we know that the planet has been through various periods of warming and cooling, most notably, there have been a number of ice ages that have then been followed by periods of warming. So why worry about a 1°C increase?

The first point to understand is that the change in average global temperatures is a measure based on a sample of temperature readings taken around the planet throughout each year. Scientists are continually measuring temperatures at locations around the globe, both on land and at sea. These measurements are compared year-on-year for the same time periods to track differences. The average of these increases/decreases gives a long-term trend. Early data on global temperatures was collected in the latter part of the 1800s, and changes in average global temperatures are measured against this initial data.

Figure 1.1: Changes in average global temperatures

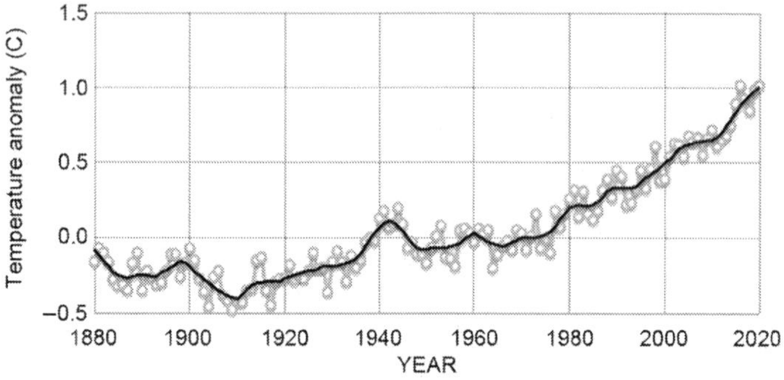

Source: NASA's Goddard Institute for Space Studies (GISS)[2]

Figure 1.1 shows the trend in average global temperatures; however, the actual temperatures in one specific area might vary significantly above or below the historical norm. For example, one region might experience unusually cold winters, while in other regions, the temperatures could be far higher than the historical norm.

The discussion on climate change invariably refers to the *average* increase in global temperatures, but it is this variation that is likely to cause the real problem for human communities and regional ecosystems. For example, in the last few years the Indian sub-continent has experienced peak summer temperatures that are up to 15°C degrees higher than they were 20 years ago. Similarly, Siberia is experiencing summer temperatures that are more than 20°C higher than recent norms, causing permafrost to melt and release huge quantities of previously trapped methane.

Is human activity to blame?

Research by John Cook et al (2013) showed that academic papers on climate change overwhelmingly endorse the view that the current dramatic increase in global warming is caused by human activity, also referred to as anthropogenic global warming (AGW). 'Among papers expressing a position on AGW, an overwhelming percentage (97.2% based on self-ratings, 97.1% based on abstract ratings) endorses the scientific consensus on AGW.'[3]

Six years later, research showed that the level of consensus among research scientists on AGW has grown to 100 per cent (based on a review of 11,602 peer-reviewed articles on climate change and global warming).[4]

However, this level of unanimity within the scientific community is not reflected within the wider population and public perceptions of climate change vary widely. Research by John Cook et al shows that: '57% of the US public either disagree or are unaware that scientists overwhelming believe that the earth is warming due to human activity.'

This lack of public understanding is due, in part, to campaigns designed to confuse the public about the causes of climate change and deliberate attempts to create an impression that there is a lack of consensus among climate scientists. Two reasons are commonly used to contradict the evidence that human activity is to blame. The first is *the earth has always gone through natural cycles that move between ice age and a more temperate climate*. The second is *the current increase in global temperatures is caused by sunspots*.

There is an element of truth in both these arguments. Clearly, the planet does go through warm and cold phases. However, these periods of natural climate change occur over thousands of years, whereas human induced climate change has occurred at an extraordinarily rapid rate with dramatic changes seen in less than 100 years. Similarly, sunspot activity may have some effects on earth's climate, but any such impact is minimal and does not account for the steady increase that has been experienced over the last 100 years.

If governments are to implement the dramatic changes required to address climate change, it will be essential to have the support of voters and consumers. The current public confusion over the causes of climate change, and indeed, perceptions that it may not be a significant threat, has to be addressed. It is imperative that the wider public understand the key issues and can make informed decisions about the political changes that will be required if we are to move towards a sustainable economic model.

Greater public concern for global warming will require an understanding of the linkage between the rise in global temperature and the causal factors such as CO_2 emissions and methane emissions. In addition, there needs to be a better understanding of the linkage between damage to the natural environment, particularly deforestation, and the risk of feedback loops.

The challenge facing humanity is to reduce carbon emissions rapidly over the next decade and to be carbon neutral before 2050. The scale of the task confronting us is enormous and it is important that there is a managed transition to renewables. We have to act now so that we avoid reaching a cliff edge where we either stop using all forms of fossil fuel, or cross the *tipping point* beyond which human intervention will be unable to reverse climate change.

The Paris Climate Conference, 2015

The 21st Conference of the Parties in Paris, 2015 (COP 21) was a landmark in international cooperation. One hundred and ninety-six countries reached consensus on the urgency to tackle climate change. Subsequently, 174 countries committed to incorporate their obligations within their own legal systems. However, while the achievement of the Paris Conference should not be underestimated, there are three main flaws:

- The parties agreed to limit global warming to well below 2°C and "pursue efforts" to limit the increase to 1.5°C. However, the ambition to "pursue efforts" is vague and leaves the door open for an increase above 1.5°C.[5]
- The signatories to the agreement set voluntary targets for future greenhouse gas emissions, not legally binding

commitments, although several countries have subsequently enshrined their goals in law.

- The collective emissions of these voluntary targets exceed the required limit on greenhouse gas emissions and current policies are projected to cause global temperatures to rise by 2–3°C.[6]

The Paris conference was an important milestone and we should not belittle the intention to reach international agreement, but equally, we should not treat the Paris Agreement as the road map that will lead us away from disaster. It was a political compromise and needs to be replaced with an agreement that legally binds nations to emission quotas that will limit global warming to 1.5°C. One of the aspirations for the 2020 Conference of Parties, which had been scheduled to take in place in Glasgow until it was cancelled due to COVID-19, was to address this issue.

One of the frustrations for observers of the annual Conference of Parties is that protecting the global economy appears to take priority over avoiding an environmental catastrophe. This frustration was summed up when Greta Thunberg was invited to address the UN Climate Action Summit. When asked what her message was to the gathering of world leaders, she said, "We will be watching you." She went on to say:

> For more than 30 years, the science has been crystal clear. How dare you continue to look away and come here saying that you're doing enough, when the politics and solutions needed are still nowhere in sight.
>
> You say you hear us and that you understand the urgency. But no matter how sad and angry I am, I do not want to believe that. Because if you really understood the situation and still kept on failing to act, then you would be evil. And that I refuse to believe.
>
> The popular idea of cutting our emissions in half in 10 years only gives us a 50% chance of staying below 1.5 degrees, and the risk of setting off irreversible chain reactions beyond human control.

Fifty percent may be acceptable to you. But those numbers do not include tipping points, most feedback loops, additional warming hidden by toxic air pollution or the aspects of equity and climate justice. They also rely on my generation sucking hundreds of billions of tons of your CO_2 out of the air with technologies that barely exist. So, a 50% risk is simply not acceptable to us: we who have to live with the consequences. (Greta Thunberg: address to the UN Climate Action Summit, 2019)[7]

The next major opportunity for world leaders to demonstrate their commitment to reduce carbon emissions will be the delayed COP 26 event, in Glasgow, November 2021. Perhaps 2021 will be the year when world leaders acknowledge that they need to place the environment ahead of the economy. With luck, we will see economic strategies designed to protect the planet, rather than environmental strategies designed to protect the economy.

2020 changed the way we live and how we work. It highlighted the divisions in society and recalibrated the value that we place on different jobs. Maybe, a post-COVID-19 world will provide an opportunity to challenge aspects of modern society previously regarded as sacrosanct, such as cheap energy, unrestricted exploitation of natural resources and mass consumerism. The threat of COVID-19 forced governments to take actions that would have been unimaginable prior to January 2020. Perhaps there has been a shift in the role of governments from promising that standards of living will improve, to reassuring their populations that their safety is paramount.

We have seen criticism of governments that have attempted to 'keep the economy going', rather than take aggressive action to control a crisis. We saw politicians offer reassurances that they were doing a great job, yet death rates climbed. We wait to see whether the same behavioural characteristics will be exhibited in November 2021 when political leaders set out their actions to control climate change.

At the time of writing, there was little information on the official government website to describe the objectives, agenda or expectations for COP 26. There is a section on a competition for young people to '… paint, draw or design a piece of art …', there is a section on 'Together for Our Planet', that proclaims "… each of us has a part to play …", but there is not much information about the scale of the challenge, the limited time available or any intention to commit world leaders to implement the radical changes required. Perhaps this is an unfair poke at a website that seeks to engage with an audience that may not be subject matter experts. But even so, it hardly offers reassurance that the event will be taking decisions to protect the future of civilization.

The need for urgent action

Our current, highly industrialized, economic model drives ever-increasing levels of production by the exploitation of the planet's natural resources. If we are to address the threat of climate change, we not only need technical change (eg electric vehicles, renewable energy, biodegradable plastics), we also need behavioural change, (eg a recognition that our societies need to be environmentally sustainable). Ultimately, it is the behaviour of individuals that will put pressure on organizations and governments to act in ways that support a sustainable global economy.

Transitioning to a sustainable economy offers huge potential for innovation, wealth creation and increases in the standard of living. Although we stand at a perilous point in human history, there are many reasons to be optimistic:

- New technologies offer cost-effective energy from renewable sources.
- Many countries are already implementing these technologies.
- There is a small but influential minority that is pushing governments to adopt environmentally responsible policies.
- The corporate sector is starting to recognize the commercial opportunities created by adopting environmentally responsible strategies.

However, we still face many barriers, particularly from within the national governments that will need to make the necessary binding, international agreements. Probably the biggest issues to be addressed are:

- The level of inertia within many national governments.
- The lack of capability within governments to manage the scale of social and economic change required.
- The ability of corporate interests to influence political policy.
- The pursuit of national self-interest.

A matter of terminology

Before going any further it might be useful to clarify our use of the terms *growth*, *development* and *sustainable*. This may seem an obsession with semantics, but an understanding of these terms is important.

Growth

Governments frequently refer to *growth* as a key objective. Growth is usually measured by the value of goods and services produced by a country, normally measured by gross domestic product (GDP). However, a single measure such as GDP tells us little about the quality of life for individuals, families or communities. Countries may show a steady growth in GDP, but at the same time there could be growing social problems such as crime, drug addiction and unemployment. A country's economy may grow, but the gap between the wealthy and the rest of society might, and frequently does, get wider.

Development

Development is concerned with a wide range of issues that we might broadly categorize as *quality of life*. In emerging economies, the goals frequently relate to issues such as better education, improved health care, reduced levels of infant mortality and improvements to agriculture. However, we need to be careful because development is often used in the context of economic development and this may have greater focus on economic growth, rather than the development of society and the quality of life. This distinction is important because intergovernment agencies such as the UN frequently adopt strategies that boost national GDP (growth) but may not necessarily address the quality of life for the poor (development).

The distinction between growth and development is particularly important for organizations such as the World Bank and International Monetary Fund (IMF). Many of their programmes within emerging economies have pursued economic growth but, in the process, might have exploited natural resources, displaced communities or transferred land ownership rights away from local communities. As a consequence, economic growth might increase, but the impact on society might be higher levels of unemployment and greater levels of inequality.

Sustainable

The third term that needs to be understood is *sustainable*. In this book, we will use the term to describe activities that avoid lasting damage to the natural environment. A sustainable economy will need to fulfil a range of requirements, for example:

- Energy produced without creating greenhouse gases.
- Industrial activity based on renewable resources and recyclable materials.
- Manufacturing and agricultural processes that avoid greenhouse gas emissions and pollution to rivers, oceans and the air.
- Economic resources sourced without destruction of the natural environment and ensure that land is managed in ways that protect ecosystems.
- Consumer goods designed so that materials can be recycled or the materials are biodegradable.

It is worth stressing that the goal for sustainable economic activity is to provide societies with standards of living that are comparable, or better than, our existing lifestyles. A sustainable economic model does not require a return to some version of a pre-industrial society. The examples listed above are not a fanciful wish list for the future but are practical options available today. The primary reason that many organizations choose not to pursue these strategies is that sustainable methods often incur additional costs. For most organizations, damage to the environment does not show up as a cost in their financial accounts yet implementing actions to mitigate environmental damage is frequently a cost that reduces profit.

The principle that organizations should operate in ways that are environmentally responsible is not new. Over the last 100 years, there has been considerable legislation designed to protect the environment and we can build on these achievements. A key principle of future policy should be that organizations are responsible for the environmental cost of their activities, the so-called *polluter pays* principle. However, many governments are reluctant to impose this type of burden on the corporate sector and therefore there has been a lack of political will to introduce polluter pays legislation. One reason for the lack of progress is that it requires international agreement to become fully effective, otherwise those countries that ignored this type of legislation would produce cheaper goods and have competitive advantage. Another reason is that exploitation of natural resources provides the primary source of wealth for some economies. Until alternative sources of wealth are available, there is little incentive to stop such activities.

Achieving international cooperation on issues such as polluter pays and agreements to stop the destruction of the natural environment will require the authority of organizations such as the UN. The next few chapters will look at the role of the intergovernmental organizations, such as the UN and World Bank and will consider how these organizations set their goals, deliver their programmes and measure their outcomes. The chapters also consider the UN's Sustainable Development Goals (SGD) and discuss the capabilities that will be required to achieve these goals.

The need for a new socio-economic model

Economic growth over the last 100 years has provided increasingly high standards of living for many parts of society, particularly within the countries with advanced economies. During this period, the damaging environmental consequences of this activity have been largely ignored, partly out of ignorance of the extent of the problems being caused but also because greater priority was given to serving the high-level goals of economic growth. We are all culpable. Governments, corporations and each of us, individually, have largely ignored the problems. We may have expressed concerns about environmental problems, but invariably we have supported the activities that create strong economies, profitable businesses and improve our quality of life. However, we can no longer pretend that the benefits of a modern, industrialized economy outweigh the environmental costs and we are confronted by the grim reality that our current economic model has to change.

The technology for the transition to a sustainable society already exists, but there will be implications for all aspects of our economy, including transport, buildings, cities, consumer goods, agriculture and energy infrastructure. It will affect the jobs that we do, the skills that we need and the way we distribute wealth. It will also require changes in our values, attitudes and behaviours. Moving to a sustainable society requires not just a change in technology but changes in the things we value and the way that we live our lives.

A key objective of this book is to identify how we, individually and collectively, can support the transition to sustainable socio-economic model, deliver the required change quickly and achieve a just and prosperous society in the process.

2

The State of the World

Chapter summary

Chapter 2 assesses the impact of human activity on the climate and the natural environment. It considers the challenge of growing populations, finite resources and consumers' expectations that they will enjoy ever-higher standards of living. The chapter also looks at the phenomenon of natural feedback loops and the interdependence between life on land and in the oceans, and changing global temperatures. It considers how a changing climate causes damage to the natural environment including implications for insects, land degradation and marine life. The final part of the chapter considers the need for international coordinated action and the challenges facing intergovernmental organizations, primarily the UN. It concludes with a summary of the potential consequences if our global industrial society continues along the current trajectory.

Introduction

It is self-evident that many of the planet's natural resources are finite, yet we continue to consume resources at an unsustainable rate. The global population is expanding rapidly and this is only going to exacerbate the pressure on natural resources. Human activity is affecting our climate, the natural environment and the intricate ecological balance that supports life on earth. Populations in countries with less advanced economies are already suffering the consequences of climate change; crops fail, communities are displaced and unemployment, poverty and hunger inevitably follow. Those in the countries with advanced economies should not assume that their greater wealth will insulate them from the consequences of climate change. The consequences will affect every one of us. It is important that individuals and communities understand what is happening, why it is happening and what they can do about it.

Cause and effect

A number of different gases cause global warming of which the primary cause is CO_2, but nitrous oxide and methane are also significant. Human activity has resulted in a dramatic increase in these gas emissions. Levels of CO_2 are increasing, while at the same time, human activity on the planet is reducing the ability of nature to absorb CO_2; tropical forests are destroyed, terrestrial biosphere is degraded and marine environments are being damaged (oceans are a major absorber of CO_2). Figures 2.1, 2.2 and 2.3 illustrate the data trends of these key determinants of global temperatures.

The level of CO_2 in the atmosphere is determined by two factors: the rate at which CO_2 is emitted and the rate at which

Figure 2.1: Key indicators correlated to climate change

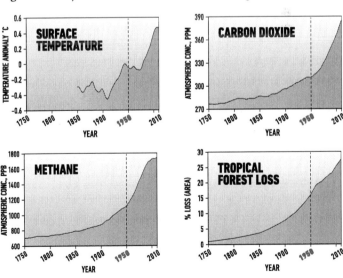

(continued)

Figure 2.1: Key indicators correlated to climate change (continued)

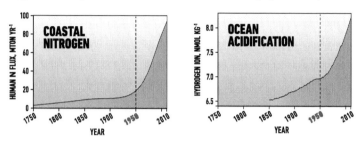

Source: Steffen, W., W. Broadgate, L. Deutsch, O. Gaffney, C. Ludwig. 2015. 'The Trajectory of the Anthropocene: The Great Acceleration', *The Anthropocene Review*.[1]

it is removed from the atmosphere. Over the last couple of centuries, human activity has dramatically increased the rate of emission and at the same time, human activity has damaged the capacity of the natural environment to absorb CO_2. A significant proportion of CO_2 is absorbed by green vegetation on land, particularly tropical rain forests, but other major absorbers of CO_2 include marine vegetation and other organisms (eg kelp and phytoplankton in the oceans).

The Telegraph (18 August 2011)[2] quoted a study by Dr Simon Lewis at the University of Leeds that calculated that the world's forests absorb 8.8. billion tonnes of CO_2 per year. The Amazon accounts for approximately 25 per cent of this figure. One of the problems of rain forest destruction is not only that the earth loses the capacity to absorb CO_2 but also it causes the release of CO_2 as the trees are burnt. Analysis by Global Forest Watch reports that:

- Loss of tropical forest accounts for 8 percent of the world's annual carbon dioxide emissions.
- If tropical deforestation were a country, it would be the third-biggest emitter globally, ranking just below the US and significantly higher than the EU.
- Between 2015 and 2017, forest-related emissions were 63 per cent higher than the average for the previous 14 years, rising from 3 billion to 4.9 billion metric tons per year. (Report published by World Resources Institute: Gibbs, Harris and Seymore, October 2018)

Destruction of forests not only reduces the capacity to absorb CO_2 but it is also destroying the habitat of animal and plant species, causing a rapid increase in the rate of extinction. The consequences of this mass extinction of species are impossible to quantify. Not only are we losing species that have the potential to benefit humanity but at a more fundamental level it is disrupting the delicate balance of food chains, causing the collapse of entire ecosystems.

Figure 2.2: CO_2 emissions from tropical forest losses

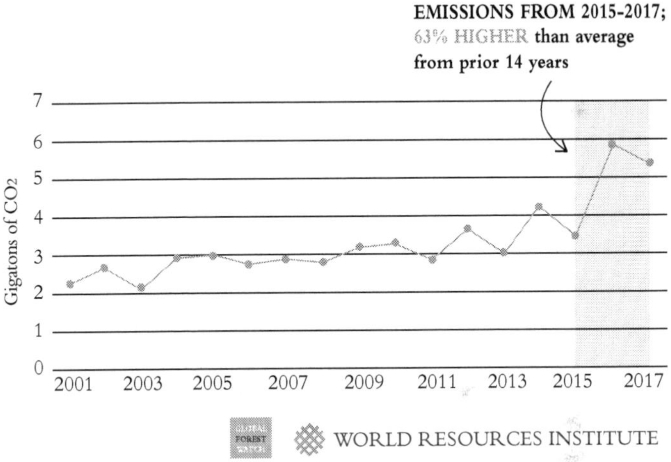

EMISSIONS FROM 2015-2017;
63% HIGHER than average
from prior 14 years

WORLD RESOURCES INSTITUTE

Note: Loss calculated at a 25% tree cover density
Source: World Resources Institute[3]

An article on the NASA Earth Observatory website states that approximately 10 gigatons (one billion tonnes) of atmospheric carbon is processed by phytoplankton per year.[4] One of the problems caused by increasing levels of CO_2 is that greater concentrations of CO_2 increase the acidity of the oceans, which in turn causes a decline in the levels of phytoplankton that are sensitive to acidity levels. The destruction of phytoplankton is exacerbated by their sensitivity to rising sea temperatures, accelerating the feedback loop.

Rising temperatures cause permafrost to melt, which in turn releases methane gas, which is many times more powerful as a greenhouse gas than CO_2. This causes a further rise in temperatures and melting of permafrost, increasing rates of release of methane and so on. As temperatures rise, the ice caps melt and this in turn reduces the ability of the planet to reflect heat from the sun and so the feedback loop of global warming continues.

Although CO_2 is the main factor driving climate change, there are other significant contributors to global warming. Methane is one of the other major factors and results partly from natural sources such as melting permafrost, but it is also produced by animal agriculture. Other factors include chemicals used in fridges and air conditioning units, known as HFCs. These are exceptionally powerful agents when released into the atmosphere, and their effect on global warming can be hundreds of times greater than CO_2, although the rate of decay will be quicker.

Figure 2.3: Combined heating influence of greenhouse gases

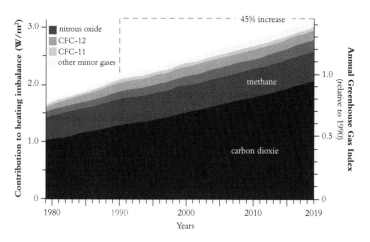

Source: Graph by NOAA Climate.gov, based on data from NOAA's Earth System Research Laboratories[5]

Understanding the science is important and unless voters are informed on these issues, they cannot be expected to support the actions of government that will be required if we are to prevent runaway global warming. At the time of writing, there was only limited public pressure for governments to take urgent action. Where governments do intervene with actions (eg congestion charges in cities or increases in fuel duty), there is the probability that the public will resist such action. For example, in 2018, the French government increased fuel duty to encourage consumers to buy more fuel-efficient vehicles, but by the end of the year, we saw violent demonstrations across France by the movement known as *gilets jaunes* (yellow vests).

By contrast, environmental policies are more likely to be accepted when the reasons are understood. When the British government introduced a charge on the use of plastic carrier bags, there appeared to be broad public support. This apparent support was probably because recent television programmes by Sir David Attenborough had raised public concern over plastic pollution in our oceans. Human activity is causing damage to most aspects of the natural environment, but there are two issues that are worth highlighting at this point: the decline of species and land degradation.

The decline of species

Climate change is causing shifting distribution, decline in animal populations and alarming rates of species extinction. Insects are the most diverse group of animals on the planet, and they are particularly vulnerable to climate change. The consequences of the decline of insects is virtually impossible to predict due to the complex interdependency between, insects, plants and animals. However, to give one simple example, the decline in bee populations means that in some parts of the world, bees have to be artificially reared to ensure pollination of agricultural crops.

The potential rates of extinction associated with different levels of climate change have been set out in a report published by R. Warren, J. Price, E. Graham, N. Forstenhaeusler, J. VanDerWal et al (May 2018).[6] The report was cited in an article published on the website of the American Association for the Advancement of Science (AAAS) and projected that, at different levels of global warming a given percentage of species will decline by more than 50 per cent. Table 2.1 shows the percentage of species that are likely to suffer more than 50 per cent losses at different levels of global warming.

These findings show that there will be significant losses across the plant and animal kingdom, with rises in global temperature rising from 1.5°C to 3.2°C.

Table 2.1: Projected decline of species at different scenarios for climate change

°C increase	% decline in species		
	Vertebrates	Plants	Insects
3.2°C	25	44	49
2.0°C	8	16	18
1.5°C	4	8	6

Source: American Association for the Advancement of Science. Report published by R. Warren, J. Price, E. Graham, N. Forstenhaeusler, J. VanDerWal, et al (May 2018).

It is worth noting that the reason why 3.2°C was selected as the upper limit was that at the time of the research, the pledges made under the Paris Agreement were estimated to result in a 3.2°C increase if the pledges were achieved. Table 2.1 shows that at 3.2°C 49 per cent of insect species will suffer a decline of more than 50 per cent.

Land degradation

The degradation of soil due to unsustainable farming practices threatens the future of agricultural land. This process is happening wherever farming uses heavy machinery and chemicals. In 2017, the Secretary of State for Agriculture, Michael Gove, warned that the UK was between 30 and 40 years away from eradication of soil fertility:

> If you have heavy machines churning the soil and impacting it, if you drench it in chemicals that improve yields but in the long term undercut the future fertility of that soil, you can increase yields year on year but ultimately you really are cutting the ground away from beneath your own feet. Farmers know that. (Speech by Michael Gove quoted in *The Guardian*, 24 October 2017)[7]

This means that if we continue with current farming practices, agriculture will no longer be capable of producing healthy, high-yielding crops. This decline in world agricultural output will coincide with a projected global population of over 10 billion by the end of this century. A report by The United Nations Convention to Combat Desertification (UNCCD) stated: Land degradation threatens the livelihoods of billions of people around the world. This is particularly the case for populations living in rural areas where most of the poor people reside: estimates report that 80% of the extreme poor live in rural areas and 65% work in the agricultural sector.

The report goes on to identify the causes: 'land degradation continues to increase worldwide due to several factors, including the expansion of crop and grazing lands into native vegetation, unsustainable agricultural and forestry practices, climate change, urban expansion, infrastructure development, and extractive industry' (UNCCD report published 2019: *Land Degradation, Poverty and Inequality*).[8]

The challenge for the UN

Climate change presents an imminent threat to our survival and we have to reduce greenhouse gas emissions dramatically, to near zero before 2050. Radical social and economic change is required. One thing is clear, the action of a few committed nations will not be sufficient; an international response is required and intervention by the various organizations of the UN will be essential. However, the track record of the UN in persuading countries to take action has, to date, been poor. For over 20 years, the UN has hosted international conferences that have resulted in various declarations and promises, but once away from the conference tables the impetus for radical action seems to fade. There are serious concerns that the UN does not have the level of influence required to achieve the changes required. While the UN is probably the right organization to take responsibility for leading a coordinated response, it currently lacks the authority to fulfil such a mandate.

The UN is undoubtedly concerned about climate change, but it seems powerless to drive radical action. At a time when the world is standing on the brink of catastrophe, the UN should be exposing the causes of global warming, yet there is a sense that the UN is wary of straying into politically sensitive areas or engaging in activities that could conflict with the aims of the major donors. The UN is heavily dependent upon the support of the major international players such as the US, Russia, China and the European nations. If support is withheld this will limit the ability of the UN to carry out its work. For example, the UN has an important role in monitoring global warming, but it is dependent upon NASA to gather scientific data. Action by the Trump administration to reduce funding to NASA's earth monitoring programme directly affected the ability of the UN to monitor global warming. An article in Sciencemag.org in May 2018 reported on the cancellation of NASA's Carbon Monitoring System (CMS):

> The move jeopardizes plans to verify the national emission cuts agreed to in the Paris climate accords, says Kelly Sims Gallagher, director of Tufts University's Center for International Environment and Resource Policy in Medford, Massachusetts. 'If you cannot measure emissions reductions, you cannot be confident that countries are adhering to the agreement,' she says.[9]

Another NASA programme that supports scientific research into climate change is also under threat. An article in the *Scientific American* comments on planned cuts by the Trump administration in the proposed budget for the US government 2021 fiscal year.

> The administration wants to eliminate funding for a NASA program that is developing an observatory to monitor Earth to better understand climate change.
> NASA's Climate Absolute Radiance and Refractivity Observatory would produce 'highly accurate and trusted climate records' that can help produce policies on mitigation and adaptation 'that address the effects of climate change on society', NASA says. The observatory is scheduled to launch in 2023.

The administration acknowledges the observatory 'would provide additional capabilities over existing satellites' but says the project 'is a lower priority compared to other NASA programs'. The administration's budget boosts funding for missions to land astronauts on the moon and Mars.[10]

The UN's activities are constrained by its relationships with international governments, particularly the major donors, and these governments are, in turn, potentially subject to the power of various interest groups. The consequence is that the UN might not act as an independent organization and its activities might risk being affected by the political manoeuvrings of the major donors.

Other reasons for the apparent impotence of the UN relate to the structures and lines of authority within the organization. The UN has built an organization with specific skills, competencies and ways of working that make it effective at delivering projects against defined outcomes. The concern is that these outcomes might be narrowly defined, such as improvement of transport infrastructure or other economic criteria, but there is a risk that a specific programme of work may not be part of a holistic approach to delivering sustainable development. In essence, the organizational structure and decision-making processes of the UN are effective at delivering defined programmes of work but may lack the internal processes to determine how individual programmes fit within a complex, economic and social, system of systems. To address such issues would almost certainly require the UN to engage in wide ranging aspects of politics and social change within the recipient countries rather than deliver defined programmes of work. The UN undoubtedly does incredible work but its current mandate, structures and capabilities do not position it to drive radical international change.

There is distinct gap between what the UN seeks to achieve and what it is empowered to achieve. A clear aspiration within the UN is to promote the conditions for a just and stable world and the vision statement by H.E. Mr Tijjani Muhammad-Bande,

President-elect of the 74th Session of the United Nations General Assembly sets out a number of priorities, including:

• Promotion of international cooperation for the consolidation of universal peace and mutual respect among all nations and elimination of discrimination in all its manifestations.
• Respect for international law and treaty obligations as well as the seeking of settlement of international disputes by negotiation, mediation, conciliation, arbitration and adjudication.
• Promotion of a just world economic order.

These are undoubtedly important aspirations and will be pursued with genuine commitment. But do those within the organization believe that the UN has the authority to achieve these outcomes? Do the managers and staff at the UN feel empowered to challenge the root causes that need to be addressed in order to achieve peace, respect for international law and a just world economic order? The UN may be committed to alleviating the suffering that exists in many parts of the world, but it is not designed to challenge the behaviour of governments or major corporations that might be creating the problems it seeks to rectify.

Limitations on the UN

Not only is the UN dependent on funding from its major donors, particularly Western governments, but much of the UN's expenditure is channelled through major corporations (eg infrastructure projects, such as energy, transport and other capital investments in the emerging economies). When these projects work well they improve the lives of people through social and economic initiatives, but not all projects deliver the intended benefits and there has been a chequered history with examples of emerging countries taking on huge debts. This in turn has resulted in the recipient countries being required to adopt economic policies that have been imposed by the intergovernmental organizations and donor countries.

One of the concerns with the UN is that its activities may be more focused on implementing programmes to address *symptoms* rather than address the *causes*. To take a simplistic example: malnutrition in developing countries is frequently a consequence of people not having work and therefore not having money to buy food. A programme to support better agricultural practice and increase yields may make farms more productive, but it will not enable the unemployed to buy food. Indeed, the changes that deliver increased productivity might displace farm labourers causing greater unemployment and poverty.

It is not surprising that the criteria for lending money to emerging economies will, to some extent, be linked to the national interests of the donor countries, however, it is important that there is transparency with regard to the stated aims of such projects, how they are being implemented and who benefits. In particular, the UN needs the ability to design programmes that address the root causes of conflict, poverty and injustice, without undue influence from donor governments. Historically, UN strategy has reflected the philosophy of many of its donor nations that economic growth is good. Going forward, it is essential that the UN focuses on programmes that deliver *sustainable development*, not simply pursue an agenda of economic growth.

The US is the biggest single donor to the UN and there was a sense that the Trump administration did not regard funding the activities of the UN as consistent with a policy of *America First*. The election of President Joe Biden in January 2021 was a pivotal moment, not just for American politics but also for the future of the planet. It provides hope that the second biggest emitter of greenhouse gases (after China) will move from a position where the impending threat of global warming had been largely dismissed, to an administration that will hopefully base policy decisions on scientific evidence. Within the first 24 hours in office, Biden signed 15 executive orders reversing key policies of the Trump administration, most notably, Biden's commitment to rejoin the Paris Agreement. The significance of the Biden victory cannot be overestimated, not just for what he will, hopefully, achieve but also for what he will prevent. The political policies enacted during 2020–2030 will determine whether we are able to limit climate change to below 2°C or not. The social, economic and political changes that will be required to reduce carbon emissions will demand a unity of international will and level of cooperation rarely seen in international politics. The ability of the US President to show leadership and direction will be fundamental to achieving such unity of purpose.

Climate change and UN agencies

There is an interesting interplay between the various agencies of the UN. Some of them directly influence the economic strategies of national economies, such as the World Bank and IMF, while other agencies are on the front line, responding to crises such as failed harvests, health pandemics and political unrest, for example, the Food and Agricultural Organization, World Health Organization and UN High Commissioner for Refugees. There is a potential contradiction if UN agencies, such as the World Bank, IMF or UN Development Programme, are implementing policies to achieve economic growth, potentially resulting in environmental problems, while other UN agencies are coping with the consequences of drought, migration and regional conflict. There is a particular problem where the UN provides economic support to drive economic growth by activities that destroy natural resources. Going forward, UN support for economic development should be contingent on effective measures to prevent damage to the natural environment. Alternatively, if the UN is guided by a philosophy that places economic growth as the priority, then it may support programmes that result in higher emissions of greenhouse gases and greater pressure on natural resources. The activities of the UN should be evaluated against *sustainable* objectives such as:

- Low carbon growth.
- Protection of natural resources.
- Protection of endangered species.
- Protection of oceans and rivers.

Sustainable development goals

One of the landmark achievements of the UN in recent years has been to define the Millennium Development Goals (MDG) and subsequently, the Sustainable Development Goals (SDG). The SDG have become a set of goals that governments can unite behind, and the corporate world frequently incorporates them within their own strategic goals.

A number of the SDG are directly related to achieving clean growth:

Goal 6: Clean water and sanitation
Goal 7: Affordable and clean energy
Goal 11: Sustainable cities and communities
Goal 12: Responsible consumption and production
Goal 13: Climate action
Goal 14: Life below water
Goal 15: Life on land

These goals set clear and practical guidance for any government or organization that seeks to incorporate sustainability within their policies or strategy. The weakness of the SDG is that they are aspirational, and the UN has little authority to demand compliance. For example, Goal 6 relates to clean water and sanitation. This high-level goal is broken down into specific examples of the actions required. For example:

Goal 6: Clean water and sanitation:
6.1 By 2030, achieve universal and equitable access to safe and affordable drinking water for all.
6.3 By 2030, improve water quality by reducing pollution.
6.6 By 2020, protect and restore water-related ecosystems, including mountains, forests, wetlands, rivers, aquifers and lakes.

Nobody could argue with the intention of the SDG, but there is little explanation as to how such intentions are enforced. The other concern with the SDG is that they do not explicitly address the risk of irreversible global warming. Perhaps there is an opportunity for the UN to define an additional set of goals, *climate change goals*, in order to focus attention on the issues being addressed by the IPCC.

Such goals might include:

- Global warming: Limit temperature increase to a maximum of 1.5°C.
- Energy sources: Stop generating energy from fossil fuels and convert to renewable sources.
- Environmental economic costing: Account for environmental damage in commercial accounting and reporting.
- Sustainable development: Economic activity to be undertaken within the boundaries of sustainable resources.
- Financial systems: Financial and monetary systems to serve the purpose of enabling sustainable economic activity.
- International economic cooperation: Support the social and economic transition of nations dependent on fossil fuels.
- Migration: Protect those displaced from their homes, lands and jobs as a result of climate change and its consequences.
- Just transition: Provide citizens and communities with social and economic support to ensure that the process of transition does not discriminate on grounds of race, ethnicity, religious belief or economic status.
- Social equity: The process of transition to be based on principles that seek equality of opportunity, access to meaningful employment and protection from exploitation.

The above list is offered as an illustration of the type of issue that might be included in any list of *climate change goals*. The purpose of any such list should be to complement the SDG and to focus attention on the causes and potential consequences of climate change.

Are we destined to fail?

The history of human existence includes many sorry tales of ignorance, greed and conflict. We cannot presume that our survival is guaranteed, indeed, it would seem inevitable that at some point our civilization will collapse. A book by William Ophuls, *Immoderate Greatness* (2012) identifies a number of characteristics associated with the collapse of civilizations, including:

- A triggering cause: For example, the impact of climate change causing drought, hunger, migration and conflict.
- Denial: A failure to acknowledge the facts until it is too late.
- Mismanaged and belated response: Failing to understand the issues and adopting responses that are, too little, too late.
- Moral decay: Characterized by the decay in its values, practice and institutions. This is particularly likely to occur where societies are divided into a wealthy elite and an underprivileged majority.
- Emergence of a demagogue promising greatness: When society fails to address its problems, the emergence of a demagogue promising simple solutions becomes more likely.

While there is little comfort to be gained by seeing these characteristics unfolding today, it does, perhaps, help us to recognize symptoms associated with different phases of social and economic collapse. By recognizing the symptoms, we might be able to take action and reverse an otherwise downward spiral.

Unfortunately, the current prognosis is not good. The scientific evidence predicts that global temperatures will continue to rise and that we are likely to breach the Paris 1.5°C target. The average global temperature is currently close to a 1°C and we are already seeing the dramatic effects on our climate including floods, droughts, record high temperatures and ever-greater destruction of our natural environment. Events that were previously considered to be *once in 100 years* are now occurring every few years. Many in the countries with emerging economies have limited resources to protect themselves against the economic consequences of natural disasters, and there is an unfolding picture of human suffering as crops fail, people face starvation, communities migrate and different cultures come into conflict, potentially leading to regional wars. These problems will not be limited to isolated groups in some distant part of the world but will have consequences that affect us all.

The direct impact of climate change on the wealthier nations has, so far, been relatively localized and the majority of their populations have been able to continue with life as normal, although communities affected by hurricane Katrina, fires in California and storm surges on the east coast of the US are still suffering. Until recently, many within the advanced economies appeared to be suffering from some form of environmental myopia and had little awareness of the impending consequences of global warming. However, there are signs that public awareness is growing and public pressure for action on climate change is likely to grow.

The need for a new socio-economic model

Our modern industrialized society depends on readily available natural resources, but as these finite resources become scarcer, our low-cost, high-consumption economic model will fail. The industrialized countries will not be able to generate economic wealth by converting cheap raw materials into consumer goods, and governments will not be able to promise wealth and prosperity. Unless the global economy finds alternative ways to generate wealth and prosperity it will enter a terminal economic decline. Even if we were not facing the threat of climate change, the current socio-economic model has to evolve, as it will not survive the pressure of growing populations and declining availability of cheap resources.

Our modern society is held together by shared values, attitudes and beliefs. As the economic model of cheap consumer goods starts to collapse, it will challenge our belief in a society that has been based on the principle that continual economic growth is the basis of happiness, freedom and democracy. Therefore, not only does the transition to a sustainable society require a shift in social values, attitudes and beliefs but also a collapse in values will trigger social disruption. The continued cohesiveness of society requires a future socio-economic that is both sustainable and unifies social values.

A new age of unrest

In many countries, we see the signs of social unrest. Communities that had previously enjoyed good incomes, comfortable standards of living and job security are increasingly angry as the lifestyle of an earlier age disappears. The causes may be many and varied, but unsustainable economic growth, an increasing wealth gap, decreasing resources and disruption caused by changes in our climate are contributing factors, and their impact will increasingly be felt over the coming decades.

As the current economic model falls apart, there is a risk that there will be a fragmentation within society and a rise in extremism. On the one hand, there will be those seeking to protect their wealth and positions of power. On the other hand, there will be those calling for a more sustainable society. There is a risk that those in power may pursue policies of authoritarianism, while those calling for climate action may engage in acts of protest as their demands for change become ever more intense. Climate change is one of the most politically polarizing issues in American politics, as highlighted by an article in *The Guardian* (May 2019):

> Climate change is now more politically polarizing than any other issue in America,' said Anthony Leiserowitz, director of the Yale program on climate change communication. 'The issue has climbed and climbed in importance for the Democratic base since the 2016 presidential election to the point that it's now a top-tier concern. We have never seen that in American politics before.
>
> And yet it's dead last for conservative Republicans. The issue has flatlined for them over the past five years. In the US, your political party is the greatest indicator to your view on climate change – more than race, age or gender.[11]

As economies emerge from the COVID-19 pandemic, it is likely that politics will become polarized between those parties that offer a return to the *old normal* and those offering a *new normal*. On the one hand, there will be those that seek to return to the social and economic world that existed before the pandemic, and on the other hand, there will be those that see the disruption caused by the pandemic as an opportunity to re-evaluate our social and economic priorities.

The tactical positioning of political parties with regard to climate change will probably be determined by:

• Their perception of voter's concerns: if it is of high concern to the electorate, then political leaders will position themselves to reflect concerns relating to climate change.
• Their ability to offer credible solutions: if a political party has answers to the problem then it will proclaim its competence, if they are devoid of credible proposals, they will seek to play down potential problems that they are unable to address.
• Their dependence on groups with vested interests in the status quo: if a political party is dependent on funding or other support from groups that have an interest in protecting an unsustainable economic model then it will seek to counter the claims of parties proclaiming that climate change is a threat.

Research by Dr Rebecca Willis found that:

> Politicians understand the need for action on climate change, but it is not straightforward for them to make the case for it. There are three main reasons for this.
> First, climate change is seen as an 'outsider' issue, i.e. not something discussed as part of the political mainstream. This means MPs may be reluctant to champion it.
> Second, politicians feel under very little pressure to act on climate change. They report limited interest from their constituents, and indicate that they need to find ways to make climate action relevant to the daily lives and concerns of the electorate.
> Third, there are practical, procedural and even psychological difficulties in responding to climate change, as large scale, long term challenges do not fit well with the daily practice of politics.[12]

It is perfectly rational that communities that had once enjoyed high standards of living should want to return to an age when they enjoyed good incomes and cheap consumer goods. The challenge for those seeking to promote a shift to a new economic model is to convince a sceptical electorate that the *old normal* has to be discarded and that any attempt to hold onto it will lead to terrible consequences. This negative message will need to be balanced with the positive message that an environmentally sustainable society is not only essential but that it is capable of meeting their aspirations for a better life.

The election of Trump has been attributed to frustration in communities that have been epitomized by the rust belt of America, where there is high unemployment and wide disillusionment with the political elite. Their sense of anger is aggravated by growing inequalities in wealth and a strong sense that the political system serves a select group within society.

There is little to suggest that current levels of inequality will be reversed under the present economic model. Indeed, the growth in inequality seems likely to continue. Social unrest seems inevitable and governments may increasingly use the police and military to suppress protests and disruption. Meanwhile, lurking in the background, political and religious extremism will exploit divisions in society, creating fear and further dividing communities. Extremist groups might use violence and intimidation to pursue their own objectives and the moderate majority might be intimidated into silence. The forces that drive this unhappy projection for our future are illustrated in Figure 2.4.

Figure 2.4 seeks to show the potential for a negative spiral of events. As we stumble through the 21st century, we face enormous threats from growing pressures on finite resources, an economic system that is unsustainable and environmental challenges that threaten life on the planet. While logic might imply that change is urgently required, we need to recognize that fear of the unknown, anger aimed at those responsible and misinformation by those seeking to protect their interests, will all conspire to increase the level of resistance to the changes that are required.

Figure 2.4: Forces of disruption

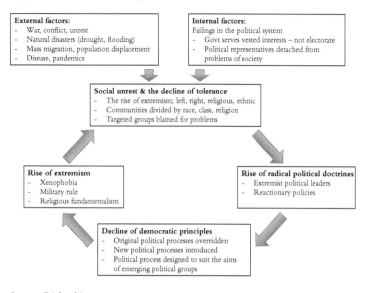

External factors:
- War, conflict, unrest
- Natural disasters (drought, flooding)
- Mass migration, population displacement
- Disease, pandemics

Internal factors:
Failings in the political system
- Govt serves vested interests – not electorate
- Political representatives detached from problems of society

Social unrest & the decline of tolerance
- The rise of extremism; left, right, religious, ethnic
- Communities divided by race, class, religion
- Targeted groups blamed for problems

Rise of extremism
- Xenophobia
- Military rule
- Religious fundamentalism

Rise of radical political doctrines
- Extremist political leaders
- Reactionary policies

Decline of democratic principles
- Original political processes overridden
- New political processes introduced
- Political process designed to suit the aims of emerging political groups

Source: Richard Joy

3

Implications of COVID-19

Chapter summary

This chapter looks at the competence of governments to respond to the COVID-19 crisis and considers the lessons we need to learn if we are to meet the challenge of climate change. It also looks at how societies have responded to new social norms and considers whether COVID-19 will be the trigger for a transition to a sustainable society.

The optimistic conclusion is that the COVID-19 crisis will result in a radical re-evaluation of our social and economic priorities, leading to changes that will enable an effective response to global warming. The pessimistic conclusion is that we will learn little and society will revert to business as usual with a desperate race to restart the global economy and return to the old normal.

Did you have a good lockdown?

Anecdotal evidence suggests that many of those in the reasonably well off middle classes have enjoyed the changes to their normal, pressurized lifestyle. The stresses of commuting and long hours in the office have been replaced by time at home and new ways of working. Some people will even offer a guilty admission that they have enjoyed lockdown. For others in society, it has highlighted their vulnerability. Many of those in insecure, low-paid jobs have been tipped into poverty within a matter of weeks, their problems exacerbated by poor housing and difficult conditions within their communities.

The fact that COVID-19 has had such different effects across society is relevant to the discussion on the process of social change because we need to understand how an event such as a pandemic or global warming, is perceived by different groups. Such events have a devastating impact on some groups, while others remain serenely insulated from the consequences. We also need to understand how governments respond in times of crisis. Could the high death rates that we have seen in so many countries been averted? What are the decision-making processes that guide government action? And, how does society respond when radical change is required?

Warning signs

It was clear from the very beginning of 2020 that COVID-19 presented a serious threat to world health. On 10 January 2020, the World Health Organization (WHO) issued comprehensive guidance on how to detect, test and manage potential cases of COVID-19.[1] The warning signs were flashing in big red letters, yet many countries were slow to respond. If there is only one lesson that we learn from COVID-19, it is that immediate action is required when a threat is growing exponentially.

On 23 January 2020 the city of Wuhan in China was put into lockdown. At that point the number of COVID-19 related deaths in China was probably less than 50, although exact figures are difficult to confirm.[2] However, it is clear that the Chinese government took drastic action to control the spread of the virus; residents were confined to their homes, and the city was sealed off from the rest of China. Within the city itself, deaths continued to rise and by mid-January 2020, the number of deaths was doubling every four to seven days. However, in spite of the news reports coming out of China, many Western countries were slow to recognize the potential threat. Where countries were slow to take action it resulted in high death rates and prolonged the time necessary to control the spread of infection. An article in *The Guardian* (11 March 2020) reported on a study into the speed of transmission of COVID-19. The article offered a summary of findings, including: 'If testing, isolation and travel bans were brought in one, two or three weeks later than they were, the number of cases could have rocketed three, seven and 18-fold respectively.'[3]

Another study by Columbia University found that if control measures had been introduced two weeks earlier, deaths in the US could have been reduced by over 80 per cent.[4]

The challenge facing governments across the world is that radical action is the only way to stop the spread of the disease, yet such action inevitably has a devastating impact on economic activity. This dilemma appears to have resulted in many governments hesitating to take action, preferring to keep the economy going and hoping that the impact of the disease could be mitigated in some way. The decision to delay taking prompt action is particularly concerning because the evidence from China had already shown that decisive action was both essential and effective. Ultimately, most governments recognized that lockdown was inevitable and that the economic consequences were unavoidable. However, concerns about disrupting the economy resulted in many countries suffering tragically high death rates before imposing the actions necessary to control the spread of the virus.

The decision to protect the economy rather than implement disruptive changes offers a direct analogy to the decisions being faced in addressing climate change. We know that global temperatures are rising and we know that we have to reduce greenhouse gas emissions, yet we continue to pursue a policy of economic growth that drives up global temperatures. The political reasoning is the same in both cases: *we don't want to disrupt the economy*. When economists review the impact of the pandemic it will be interesting to see whether those countries that reacted promptly suffered greater or lesser long-term economic consequences than those countries that attempted to keep their economies going. It might be the case that those countries that responded early suffered lower long-term economic costs than those that responded late.

The same determination to protect economic growth is delaying our response to climate change, but we are deluding ourselves if we believe that we can continue as normal. The longer we delay, the greater the problem becomes, the higher the economic costs and the more difficult it will be to resolve.

Evidence-driven decision-making

The ability to monitor and interpret data is essential in enabling governments to respond to potential threats. If the data is wrong, or the interpretation of the data flawed, or if the findings are disbelieved or ignored, then governments will respond inappropriately to the risks that confront them. Similarly, if the electorate is provided with data that underestimates the extent of a problem, then public pressure for action will be less urgent than if the full extent of the problem was known. This has implications for all government policy, but the consequences are particularly dramatic for issues such as COVID-19 and climate change.

In the UK, the Chief Medical Officer announced the first death in England on 5 March 2020.[5] By the end of July, the UK official government figures showed that there had been approximately 45,000 deaths. There has been discussion over the accuracy of this figure as UK government statistics up to the end of April did not include deaths in care homes, one of the major areas where deaths occurred. Another potential cause for discrepancy is that some COVID-19 related deaths may not have been counted if the person had not been *tested* for COVID-19. The situation was further confused in August 2020 when the methodology for recording COVID-19 deaths was changed to exclude deaths that occurred more than 28 days after the patient was first tested.[6] This gave an apparent reduction in the death rate (approximately 12 per cent of COVID-19 patients die more than 28 days after they first test positive). However, there is an argument that this change does avoid the risk that someone who had been tested for COVID might die from another cause at some point in the future. Clearly, it is difficult to arrive at a single figure that gives a true figure for any statistical measure; however, it is important that the intention is to understand the scale of the problem, not to minimize it.

Although it may be difficult to establish a consistent measure of reporting across all countries, one thing is clear: some countries have taken effective action to successfully prevent high death rates, while others have not. As at October 2020 there were a number of countries with very low death rates, these included those shown in Table 3.1.

Table 3.1: Countries with low death rates

Country	Deaths
New Zealand	25
Vietnam	35
Australia	907
China	4,634

Delayed and ineffective response

On 11 February 2020, the BBC reported that China had deployed a phone app that enabled effective track and trace to control the spread of the virus.[7] The ability of China to deploy track and trace, together with effective quarantine measures, enabled it to bring the epidemic under control in about three months, and total reported deaths after eight months was claimed to be 4,500.

The experience of China demonstrated that effective control measures could prevent the spread of the disease. In the UK, the necessity for an effective track and trace was recognized early and the British government launched an initial trial on the Isle of Wight on 7 May 2020. An article in *The Guardian* (18 June 2020) stated: '[Matt] Hancock had been particularly enthusiastic about the NHS app and had at one point said it would be "rolling out in mid-May" across England.'[8]

The initial trials ran into technical problems and the government subsequently announced that it would launch the mobile app in September 2020, but as this deadline approached, the government conceded that further delays were expected and when questioned on exactly when it would be available, the government's response was: 'The app is progressing and we will launch it when the time is right. I am not going to put a date on it...' (*The Independent*, 10 June 2020).[9]

The reasons for the delay in launching an effective phone app are not completely clear, however, technology is only part of the solution and there are multiple issues that governments need to manage if track and trace is to be effective. Some of these requirements are *technical* requirements; others relate to *health services*, others relate to *social compliance*.

41

The essential principle of the phone app is that it identifies whom an infected person has come into contact with, so that those at risk of contracting the disease can be notified and instructed to isolate. The phone app would show *red* when someone is required to isolate and *green* when they are not subject to restrictions.

The phone app also provides a mechanism to restrict people from mixing in public spaces. For example, people would *only* be allowed into public spaces if their status is *green*. But preventing people who may have the infection from accessing public spaces will require the capability to ensure compliance (eg shops might need someone to check whether a person has a *green* status on their phone before entering a shop). Therefore, technology is only part of the solution. Table 3.2 illustrates the requirements for an effective track and trace system, categorized by technical, health and social factors.

Table 3.2: Requirements for an effective track and trace capability

Technical requirements	
Requirement	**Description**
Track	The technology fulfils the required design criteria, including the capability to detect other phone users within a given radius, proximity to other users and ability to record the user's location at each point in time
Trace	Instant notification messages to all those who came into contact with an infected person, plus notification to relevant medical monitoring systems
Data storage and interrogation	Effective systems to collect/store/interrogate data from all users
Data privacy	Clear control on how data is used and how long retained, for example, data erased on a rolling 28-day basis
Data security	Robust mechanism to ensure that data will only be used for the intended purposes
Display status (red, amber, green)	User's phone to show status. For example, *green* status indicates that there has been no contact with a person known to have tested positive

Table 3.2: Requirements for an effective track and trace capability (continued)

Health services

Requirement	Description
Testing: availability	Immediate access to medical hotline if exhibiting COVID-19 symptoms
Testing: results	Rapid process of testing and notification of results
Quarantine	Any person testing positive to be required to quarantine
Patient monitoring	Medical team contact or visit each patient every few days to monitor infection and patient welfare

Social compliance

Requirement	Description
Demonstrate green status	Require phone user to show *green* before being admitted to public areas such as buildings, shops or public transport
Check and restrict	Effective mechanisms in place to check phones before entering buildings. This would require some form of check before people enter public areas and the ability to restrict those that fail the checks
Isolation	Those who have been in contact with an infected person are required to be tested immediately and then isolate for a given period of time with final testing at end of isolation
Restriction on those failing to use track and trace	Individuals not permitted to enter buildings, use public transport or be away from their home unless carrying a phone with the app
Unambiguous communications	Clear and unambiguous communication to ensure citizens understand and comply with requirements
Registration	All users required to register relevant personal details

Source: Richard Joy

Table 3.2 illustrates that there are a set of requirements for a track and trace system to be effective. Simply deploying a phone app will not be sufficient. In a society where it is possible to impose tight restrictions on social behaviour, then these types of measures can be effective. In more libertarian societies, persuading people to adopt such restrictive measures is likely to be more difficult.

Implementing an effective response to COVID-19 is a relatively simple task compared to implementing an effective response to climate change. With COVID-19, there is a single cause and the mechanisms that determine the spread of the disease are relatively simple and well understood. In addition, the impact of COVID-19 is relatively confined; clearly, it is dangerous for humans, but the other forms of life on the planet are largely unaffected. Fortunately, international effort by medical researchers resulted in the development of vaccines within extremely rapid timelines and methods for protecting against the virus were available in less than 12 months.

The challenges facing us with climate change are, by comparison, many times greater. The factors that regulate the climate are infinitely more complex. There is not a single solution to the problem and there certainly is not going to be a simple solution in the short term.

Climate change affects not just humans but the survival of life on earth as we know it, and reversing it will require a complete transformation of our carbon-based economies, the way we live and probably, the political processes that govern how a global society makes decisions. If governments struggled to make effective decisions when faced with COVID-19, there is serious doubt as to whether they will be able to respond to the threat of climate change.

The ability to anticipate a potential threat is one of the basic capabilities of any government, whether this might be a pandemic, extreme weather, terrorist attacks or climate change. In the UK, the government regularly undertakes activities to assess the UK's preparedness for such eventualities. In 2016, various government departments and related agencies took part in an exercise to assess the UK's preparedness for a flu pandemic. Known as Exercise Cygnus, it involved 950 officials from central and local government in three days of simulation to test the UK's readiness in the event of a pandemic. One of the report's findings was that care homes were likely to be at particular risk and that the NHS in general would be overwhelmed. *The Guardian* quotes a section from the report: 'The lack of joint tactical level plans was evidenced when the scenario demand for services outstripped the capacity of local responders, in the areas of excess deaths, social care and the NHS.'

Another key finding highlights that there was a lack of central government oversight: 'The UK's preparedness and response, in terms of its plans, policies and capability, is currently not sufficient to cope with the extreme demands of a severe pandemic that will have a nationwide impact across all sectors, …'.[10]

In due course, there will be an analysis of the UK government's handling of the COVID-19 crisis and perhaps the most significant point of failure will be the government's slow response to the early warning signs of a potential global pandemic in January 2020. The same is true for climate change; the evidence is available, the consequences of failing to act in time are understood, yet governments around the world are failing to act with sufficient urgency.

Hyperbole and self-delusion

In times of crisis, we expect clear and decisive leadership. In particular, we expect our governments to assess the threat, evaluate options and make the important decisions necessary to protect us. The problem that governments face is that they may have little capacity for effective decision-making in situations of complexity or uncertainty. (Complexity being defined as: the questions being known but the answers being unknown. Uncertainty being defined as the questions being unknown and the answers being also unknown.) In such situations, we would expect politicians to seek advice from relevant experts, and once consulted, have the capacity to understand the implications of different options. The process of government works less well when politicians fail to understand the seriousness of the problem, seek advice from those that mirror their own views, adopt recommendations that fit their perception of the appropriate solution and select options that are convenient to their political narrative.

During the early months of the COVID-19 crisis, the UK government held daily news conferences to update the public on the measures that were being taken to control the virus. There were frequent references to the government's commitment to follow '… the scientific advice.' The problem with this statement is that scientific advice can differ. A range of advice could be offered, but a government might select the advice that best fits its political priorities. For example, if the political priority is to protect the economy, governments might select the scientific advice that offers the least disruption to economic activity.

At some point, politicians have to make a decision and maybe we should not be surprised if politicians suffer from a tendency towards a belief in their own abilities to make such decisions. However, good decision-making is unlikely to be associated with hubris. At a time when tens of thousands of people are dying there is a particular concern if governments proclaim that they are doing '… a great job', or some similar statement. When this happens, it is difficult to know whether politicians are unaware of their failings and genuinely believe that they are doing a great job or whether they are trying to reassure a worried public. Of greater concern is the possibility that politicians might know that things are going wrong but believe that they can control the narrative.

Government ideology and paradigms

One of the characteristics of Western democracy is that political parties align themselves with particular ideologies. In many ways, this helps the political process as it enables voters to understand what different parties stand for, their values and their rationale for creating a particular sort of society. However, there is a risk that parties can become so focused on their ideology that they fail adapt to changing circumstances. For example, a right-wing ideology might incorporate concepts such as; a free market achieves the best economic outcomes; personal wealth is an incentive that drives economic growth; the *trickle-down* effect enables wealth to benefit all. Whether these statements are true or false is almost irrelevant; the real concern is that ideologies are a simplified interpretation of a complex world and should not become a justification in themselves.

As we enter an era where climate change threatens our survival, it is important that rigid ideology does not determine political policy. The rationale for decisions needs to be clear and it is increasingly important that governments are transparent about how decisions are being made, the evidence that has been evaluated and the likely consequences of their actions.

The risk that governments might make poor decisions is even greater if those making political decisions are selected for their adherence to the values and ideologies of the leadership group. While cabinet government requires consensus on key areas of policy, governments that actively block ideas will risk the pitfalls of *groupthink*, a phenomenon that has been well documented since the Bay of Pigs fiasco in 1961.

Social change

Within the first six months of 2020, the COVID-19 crisis had caused dramatic changes in UK society. It challenged people to re-evaluate the value that was placed on different roles, such as health workers, those that ensured food distribution networks continued to function, and other key roles within society. It also led many people to consider the things that they valued about their lives, their priorities and aspirations. Many acted to support their communities as the inequalities in society became more evident. One consequence of lockdown may be that it helped bring some parts of society closer together and although this effect may be transitory, it is reassuring to see how concern for others comes to the fore in a crisis.

The pandemic has triggered a range of changes in society, and each change in turn has consequences. For example, during 2020 we saw a dramatic shift towards online shopping. This resulted in significant disruption for the retail trade with shops closing, thousands of staff being made redundant and major brands filing for bankruptcy. Other sectors have had similar experiences, particularly in travel and hospitality. Businesses that were successful in January 2020 were struggling for survival six months later.

The COVID-19 crisis has also had a fundamental impact on the world of work. Those that have been lucky enough to work from home will have enjoyed the benefits of not commuting and having more time with family. Many employees will be hoping that working from home will become the new normal, and many organizations will be re-evaluating their expenditure on office overheads. Offices may become a place that employees occasionally visit rather than a regular place of work. Although this shift to virtual working was already starting to happen, changes that might have taken a decade have been compressed into a few months. Organizations that might have resisted losing control of their workers have seen that their employees continue to work productively from home and that there is less time spent unproductively travelling to business meetings, and there is reduced expenditure on business travel.

Organizations are likely to implement new ways of working, and expensive office space might become a corporate luxury rather than a business necessity. As a consequence, the demand for office space could collapse and this could have a ripple effect throughout the economy, not least because pension funds hold a high proportion of their investment in property and many companies will have balance sheets that are propped up by the value of their property holdings.

Our whole conception of the world of work has been challenged. Indeed, the very nature of the relationship between employer and employee is changing. Many traditional business relationships have been based on the principle that workers need to be *managed*, but this is now changing to a relationship based on trust and an expectation that employees want to do the best job possible. However, this in turn creates new stresses on employees who may feel a greater need to prove that they have been working. As the nature of management changes, it is likely that the skills required to be an effective manager will also change in a post-COVID world.

As the world of work changes, there is a risk that there could be further increases in social inequality. Those in well-paid jobs will have the freedom to live in their rural idyll rather than be restricted to locations close to their employer, frequently within the big cities. They will avoid the costs of commuting and they may benefit from a cash windfall when they sell their expensive city properties and move to the country, assuming that their own property prices don't fall.

On the other hand, those in low-paid manual or semi-skilled jobs may not have the same advantages. They may work in conditions where exposure to the virus continues for some years, they may need to commute daily on public transport and risk close contact with others. The inequality gap may grow bigger and discrepancies between lifestyles further exaggerated. As we emerge from the immediate impact of the crisis, we are likely to see significant sectors of society facing unemployment. We could see large numbers of people evicted from their homes, facing poverty and suffering the misery that follows.

Many countries will have businesses facing bankruptcy and economies on the brink of recession. Governments across the world will have to implement bailout strategies to protect the economy, rescue key industries and meet growing demands on social services. Individual nations will see a dramatic increase in their national debt and at the same time, it may be difficult to raise funds on the international markets. As a consequence, governments may start printing money to fund public expenditure at a time of collapsing tax revenues.

Governments will face difficult choices with regard to which industry sectors to support and how to fund growing pressures on public services. Those choices will determine which parts of society benefit and which parts carry the cost. Hopefully, these decisions will be underpinned by a long-term strategy for transitioning to a green economy and a vision for a more equitable society.

With luck, governments will avoid the discrepancies that followed the 2008 financial crisis when certain sectors of the economy were bailed-out (notably the financial sector), while other parts of society were offered little or no support. The intention behind the financial recovery in 2008 was primarily to get the economy back on its feet, and money was pumped into the financial sector with little constraint on how this money would be used.[11] The financial sector recovered quickly and soon reverted to business as normal, as a paragraph from *Prosperity without Growth* (Tim Jackson, 2017) illustrates. 'As early as December 2008, Goldman Sachs paid out $2.6 billion in end-of-year bonuses in spite of its $6.0 billion dollar bailout by the US government, justifying these on the basis that they helped to "attract and motivate" the best people' (Tim Jackson, 2017 *Prosperity without Growth: Foundations for the Economy of Tomorrow*, Chapter 2).

Structural economic change

The commercial viability of many industry sectors is likely to be threatened by changes in social behaviour. For example, rail transport requires a given volume of passengers to be economically viable, but if the concept of the office commuter no longer exists then rail travel becomes less viable. Similarly, the economic life of cities relies heavily on office workers, but many city businesses will struggle to survive if people work from home. Therefore, the complex interdependencies of *the old normal* will be disrupted.

The COVID-19 pandemic is likely to trigger structural economic changes as major industry sectors are impacted by a changing society. During 2020, we saw the short-term impact on many of parts of the economy, and it is likely that there will be lasting implications for some industry sectors. These sectors include:

- Property sector.
- Travel industry.
- Hospitality.
- Aircraft industry.
- Retail.

One of the biggest choices to be faced by governments will be whether they should accelerate the transition to a new, low carbon economy, or whether they should return to a pre-COVID-19 economy.

Economic recovery

As we emerge from the COVID-19 crisis, the priority for most governments will be to get people back into jobs and enable the economy to get back to normal. However, this must be seen as a short-term objective, not a long-term goal. If governments simply aspire to return to *the old normal* then they will fail to grasp a unique opportunity to encourage a process of social and economic transformation. At the heart of any strategy for recovery must be a desire to achieve a society that is environmentally sustainable, resilient to disruption and addresses the injustices facing many in society.

It might seem idealistic and impractical to attempt to create a new vision for society as we emerge from the COVID-19 crisis, but this type of radical recovery programme has been managed successfully before. In the period 1933–1938, Franklin D. Roosevelt enacted *The New Deal* to guide the US economy out of the Great Depression by creating new jobs. It identified a range of programmes to stimulate economic recovery and build the foundation for a fairer society. The list of programmes included:

- The National Recovery Administration (NRA), which introduced minimum wages, set maximum hours and protected worker's rights.
- The Civilian Conservation Corps (CCC), which created hundreds of thousands of jobs in environmental projects, including reforestation and flood defences.
- The Public Works Administration (PWA), which created jobs through a national construction programme: public buildings, roads, bridges and subways.
- The Agricultural Adjustment Administration (AAA), which offered support to farmers by raising prices and providing subsidies.
- The Federal Deposit Insurance Corporation (FDIC), which offered saver protection on their bank deposits and protected the public from fraudulent stock market practices.

The concept of the *Green New Deal* (discussed later in the book) offers a blueprint for transitioning to an environmentally sustainable society and its parallels with Roosevelt's strategy provide a reminder that radical social and economic change has been managed before.

Entering a post-capitalist era

There is an urgent need to formulate a new economic philosophy as continuing with free-market, neo-conservative economic models will not deliver an economic recovery that is environmentally sustainable or socially equitable. The opportunity to transition to a fairer, greener society is within our grasp but radical change would require the power of vested interests to be broken, otherwise we will return to an economic system that is based on profit maximization through the exploitation of natural resources. Let's be clear; this book is *not* about preventing successful and profitable business. This book is about ensuring that successful and profitable businesses can continue beyond the next couple of decades.

A market economy can only be sustainable if it accounts for the environmental consequences of its activities. For this to happen, there has to be greater emphasis on corporate purpose, specifically the desire to create value for society and acknowledge accountability for the environment. As we emerge into a post-COVID-19 world, we have a unique opportunity to build a green economy; however, green growth is not simply a matter of encouraging the switch to electric cars or building more wind farms; it will also require a new economic philosophy that offers an alternative to free-market forces and the values that underpin the traditional capitalist economic model. At present, there is little clarity as to what a post-capitalist economy would look like, although concepts such as *ethical capitalism* are being increasingly discussed. In an article by Kerry-Anne Mendoza in OpenDemocracy.net, there is a paragraph that captures the essence of much of this discussion: 'Supporters of capitalism might ask "why should people not benefit financially from their skills and capabilities?" Yet it could equally be asked of capitalism, "why would you penalise people for collaboration?" or "why would you incentivise behaviour which holds us back?"'[12]

If we are to evolve from the current economic model then we have to develop a robust philosophy for a post-capitalist world. The history of humanity is determined by our beliefs and perceptions of the world around us. In earlier times, society was frequently reshaped by emerging, and frequently conflicting, religious beliefs (Confucius, Judaism, Christianity, Islam, The Crusades, Protestantism, the Pilgrim Fathers). As we entered the 20th century, it was reshaped by ideas relating to society and economics (Marxism, fascism, communism, Keynesianism, monetarism). It is not clear whether changes within society prompted the emergence of new ideas or whether the new ideas triggered social change. What is clear is that an emergent, sustainable society will require theories, values and philosophies that are consistent with a sustainable society.

The COVID-19 pandemic has simply pre-empted a crisis that was inevitably going to happen as humanity suffers ever-greater disruption from growing populations, declining resources and climate change. We are entering a new world where many aspects of our lives will change and many of the values that underpinned society will be called into question. At a personal level, we are questioning whether we need to go into an office to work. At a business level, we are questioning the resilience of supply chains. At a corporate level, we are questioning the impact of structural changes in core industry sectors. At an ethical level, we are questioning the value that we put on different roles within society.

The COVID-19 virus is enabling us to rethink how we live our lives and it provides an opportunity to define what a future society might look like. The real question is *Who will determine what the new normal will look like?* Social and economic change is inevitable, and the next political battleground is likely to be fought over who determines the new economic model and who benefits from it. The transition to a sustainable society will require micro-economic theories that place greater value on social and environmental benefits rather than theories based on profit maximization. It will require mechanisms that account for environmental cost in the price of goods and services. It will require macro-economic theories that enable nations to achieve high employment, high standards of living and the benefits of international trade in ways that are sustainable.

Business theories will need to be rewritten. The pursuit of market share, the principle of economies of scale and the drive to maximize shareholder return are likely to be inconsistent with environmental responsibility. Globalization may become less viable in a world where international supply chains are at risk, and the environmental cost of shipping is included within the price. Perhaps one of the consequences of the COVID-19 crisis will be to trigger changes that strengthen small businesses and local communities. During 2020 local communities responded by establishing self-help groups, and local businesses adapted to serve customers in innovative ways. The emergent world might see greater emphasis on local and regional businesses and less dependency on interdependent global supply chains.

The prevailing economic philosophy in many Western countries since the 1980s has been loosely categorized as neo-conservatism. During periods of economic downturn government financial policies focused on *austerity* rather than government funded growth. Ironically, within the UK, the political debate frequently saw the Conservatives taunt Labour with accusations that their policies required *magic money trees*. Remarkably, as the COVID-19 forced us to stare into the abyss of economic meltdown, the UK Conservative government initiated public spending at a rate far greater than anything proposed by the far left policies of the Labour party under Jeremy Corbyn. Faced with ever-narrowing choices, the Conservative government initiated a bold economic policy to protect the economy during lockdown, but it has placed a huge burden on public sector finances. In August 2020, the national debt was greater than GDP.[13]

COVID-19 created a crisis that triggered virtually unprecedented levels of state intervention as the UK government recognized that it had to prevent a spiral of collapse and the Conservative government is to be credited for its swift economic intervention.

COVID-19 has shown that governments can implement rapid change when confronted by a significant threat and maybe one of the lessons from the COVID-19 pandemic is that voters can accept radical change if they understand why it is important. But electoral support is a fickle commodity, and a collapse in voter support can happen suddenly. In the UK, the Conservative government saw a dramatic fall in support. According to a Poll of Polls survey, the proportion of the electorate that support the Conservatives dropped from a high point of 51 per cent at the end of March 2020 to 42 per cent by the middle of August 2020.[14]

The US offers another example of a dramatic backlash when President Trump saw a collapse in his support as a result of his handling of the COVID-19 crisis. An article on the *Forbes* website (19 August 2020) reported on an opinion poll that found

68 per cent of Americans were embarrassed by the haphazard response to the crisis.[15]

The COVID-19 pandemic provides politicians with some important lessons: firstly, that an exponential problem requires a rapid response as indecision and delay allow the problem to grow rapidly, making it increasingly more difficult to deal with; secondly, it has shown that people will accept radical change when they understand the reasons for it, particularly if their safety is threatened; thirdly, public opinion places safety as a higher priority than the economy, and voters will quickly turn against a government that fails to protect its people.

Summary of key issues

Attempting to foretell the future is always going to be difficult, but the following list attempts to highlight some of the challenges that we will face.

- Neither the UK economy, European economies nor the wider global economies are sufficiently resilient to exit from the COVID-19 crisis without major social and economic disruption.
- All countries are likely to incur significant national debt.
- Less developed countries are likely to exit in a state of social and economic turmoil, potentially leading to civil unrest and regional conflict.
- Securing a global economic recovery will require unprecedented levels of international cooperation, leadership and consensus on a vision for a new global economic model.
- The structure of global trade is likely to be disrupted by the aftereffects of COVID-19, and this may be further affected by trade wars (notably between US and China) and the impact of Brexit.
- The state of the world post-COVID-19 should not be expected to return to normal.
- The relationship of corporate organizations with their employees, the environmental impact of their activities and the ethics that drive their commercial behaviour are being challenged.

- The political and economic ideologies that have driven the global economy for the last 50 years are under scrutiny.
- As society emerges from COVID-19, it will require economic philosophies that are aligned with new visions for society and economic purpose.

Two alternative scenarios for a post-COVID-19 world

With luck, we will emerge from the COVID-19 pandemic with a recognition that we have the capability to archive rapid social change. The legacy of the pandemic may be that it creates a desire to address many of the failings in our society, including a desire to live more sustainably. We might recognize that social and economic change is not only possible but also desirable.

A less optimistic view is that government, business and society rush to return to the old normal. The opportunity to achieve a green economic recovery may slip from our grasp. The lessons that we might have learnt about decision-making in a crisis might be lost in a fog of obscurity and desire to avoid recriminations. Politicians may seek to present their handling of the crisis as a success and fail to investigate how things could have been handled better. The desire for rapid economic recovery might override the desire to account for the cost of growth on the environment. Ultimately, it comes down to this: COVID-19 will cause an economic blip that might last a decade or two, whereas climate change threatens the survival of humanity on the planet. Any strategy for exiting the COVID-19 induced economic slump requires a long-term perspective that will deliver a sustainable future, not a short-term fix that extends the trajectory towards climate disaster.

PART II

The Process of Change

Part II of this book considers the forces that will help drive the transition to a sustainable society. It also considers the competencies that will be required to manage a process of social, economic and technological change.

One of the themes in Part II is that technological change is likely to be the easy bit. The real challenges are likely to be achieving changes in societal behaviours and in our political systems.

The transition to a sustainable society will also require changes in the relationship between governments and the politically influential organizations that have vested interests in avoiding a radical shift away from the status quo. The problem is not simply that major corporates may refuse to adopt more sustainable practices but rather that many of them may wish to limit the pace of change to ensure a good rate of return on their current assets.

This desire to protect existing sources of wealth is also determining the strategies of national governments and their response to climate change, particularly the oil dependent states. A report by *Carbon Tracker* (February 2021) highlights the projected impact on many nations, resulting in a multi-trillion dollar collapse in government revenues over the next couple of decades. Those states most dependent on oil are likely to lose up to 40 per cent of government revenues during this time.

Achieving a rapid transition to a low carbon global economy will require intergovernmental mechanisms to support those nations currently dependent on oil revenues. Similarly, economic intervention will be required by individual national governments to manage the impact of restructuring on their major industrial sectors.

The interdependency between different systems was highlighted in a report by the IPCC, titled *Towards a Sustainable and Resilient Future*. Chapter 8, Box 8.1 includes the following quote: 'Transformation involves fundamental changes in the attributes of a system, including value systems; regulatory, legislative, or bureaucratic regimes; financial institutions; and technological or biophysical systems.'

Managing the process of global social and economic change is going to require the abilities to manage change across multiple interdependent systems, cope with detail complexity and manage dynamic complexity. It will be difficult.

4

Preparing for Change

Chapter summary

Chapter 4 considers the changes that will be required if we are to transition to a sustainable society. It explores how we can move away from an economy based on mass consumption and the destruction of the natural environment. It looks at the implications that this will have for commercial organizations and for society in general. Such changes will require a shift in social attitudes and behaviours.

Successful change will require reforms to our current political processes and most importantly, it will require political leaders to offer a positive vision for the future. It will also require changes to the way that we measure economic success so that we place less emphasis on material wealth and more on social well-being. Society faces a choice: either it has to change by evolving a new socio-economic model, or it will have to face the consequences of climate change. However, if we get things right there is an opportunity to address the causes of climate change and in so doing, deliver a better society.

Towards a new socio-economic model

Our current industrialized economic model is unsustainable and requires a radical reappraisal of our social values and the way we live our lives. It will also require changes in the technologies that drive our economies and in the values that underpin our societies. Technical change, such as energy from renewables, will probably be the easy bit. We already have the technical capability to generate our energy from wind and solar and there will soon be effective ways to store energy so that we can cope with peaks and troughs in supply. The cost of renewables is falling dramatically and we are entering a new era of cheap, clean energy.

Changes to our social values may prove far harder. We need to change our patterns of consumption, the way we work and how we live our lives. For example, traditional vehicle ownership is characterized by an individual purchasing a vehicle, keeping it for their sole use and then selling the vehicle. Vehicles are disposable consumer goods that use significant resources from the planet and are costly to own. In future, vehicles may be owned and maintained by the manufacturer and rented to users for short periods. The cost of maintenance and end-of-life costs might be the responsibility of the manufacturer, encouraging car designs that are long lasting, sustainable and cost effective to use. A manufacturer called *Riversimple* is championing this business model. The principles behind their business are explained on their website.[1]

> We'll never sell a car as a product. We offer mobility as a service. For a fixed monthly fee our customers will receive a car – their car – and all the maintenance, insurance and fuel to run it. One payment to cover everything – at the equivalent monthly cost of running a normal, average car. We believe that this product-as-service concept could change how the world uses and values its reducing resources. It aligns our business interests with the environment's. That is why we are adopting it right through our supply chain.

Encouraging consumers to adopt new behaviours will be difficult unless there are clear benefits to consumers. Similarly, producers of vehicles may resist this *product-as-service* model as they generate turnover and profit by encouraging a *consumption-disposal* model of vehicle use. Our existing perceptions of a healthy economy and quality of living are closely linked with ideas of high consumption and rapid disposal of products as it creates profit and contributes to economic growth. If we are to become sustainable, we need to change the measures that we use to assess the benefit that consumers gain from the goods they buy. That way we measure the health of our national economy and how we account for the environmental costs of economic activity.

For example, the actual cost of vehicle ownership is high (an expensive asset sits unused for much of the time, depreciation is rapid and maintenance costs are high). GDP is boosted when consumers buy expensive cars that are costly to maintain, and we fail to account for the environmental damage caused by the extraction of raw materials and the emission of greenhouse gases.

An alternative model of car ownership might see vehicles as a shared community resource with some form of car-pooling. This is likely to become a reality as we see greater use of electric powered, autonomous vehicles so that, rather than owning a car, consumers would request a vehicle, for example, via a phone app, to pick them up from home, take them to the shops and then run them home again. The use of artificial intelligence would optimize the journeys of fleets of vehicles, and journeys might be shared with other people taking a similar route (The principles would be analogous to Uber ride sharing).

The examples above illustrate how consumer behaviour, social values and economic activity need to respond to technological changes. Advancements in technology are only commercially viable if there is demand for the products and services; in the case of consumer goods, this means that there has to be a desire to own the product. Market forces will be important in driving this transition; however, there will also be a role for government in encouraging changes in consumer behaviour. In addition, governments will need to create the business environment necessary for commercial decisions to be taken with confidence. For example, governments may encourage the switch to electric vehicles (EV), through the use of tax incentives to consumers. This will give confidence to manufacturers that there will be a rapid growth in demand for electric vehicles. Similarly, governments should set guidelines and introduce regulations to ensure that the infrastructure for EV is in place. For example, regulations relating to new house building might stipulate that all garages should incorporate EV charging points and town planning regulations might set guidelines for dedicated parking for EV. At its heart, the role of government is to provide a long-term strategy for the transition to a sustainable economy. Inevitably, this will involve regulations, legislation and fiscal policy but the emphasis should be on enabling market forces to guide the transition to a sustainable economy.

Changing attitudes and behaviours

While most of us would probably say that we want to protect the planet, in practice our support for a sustainable future is dependent on maintaining a comfortable way of life. We still want to heat our homes, go on holiday and eat the things we like. Research by supermarkets has shown that consumers will respond to questionnaires by stating that they want products that are locally produced and sustainably sourced. However, the evidence of spending patterns suggests that price is the overriding factor in determining consumer purchases. It is inevitable that producers will respond to this demand by producing the products that people want to buy and this is largely influenced by price.

Although some organizations do create innovative products to meet latent demand, most organizations will respond to current consumer demand. Therefore, changing consumer attitudes and behaviours will be essential. This change will only come about when:

- Consumers understand the linkage between their actions and the impact on the planet.
- Consumers are offered desirable alternative to the products and services that are causing environmental damage.

- The cost differential of alternative products/services is negligible, or at least, any additional cost is reflected in additional benefits and value.

Creating a vision for a sustainable future

If our social and economic models are to change, we need to have some sense of what the future should look like. Unfortunately, the track record of politicians offering a vision for the future does not offer much reassurance that the reality will match the claimed vision. The recent experience of the UK Brexit referendum illustrates the gap that can exist between aspirational vision and reality. At the time of writing, the UK had just completed its exit from the EU. It appears that we are heading towards a different outcome than the picture that was offered by those advocating the benefits of *leave* prior to the vote. There was little reference to the complex challenges to be addressed, and any concerns were discounted as a *few bumps in the road*, or some similar reassurance. Much of the recent public debate has been characterized by meaningless analogies and vague promises, but there is little accountability if the reality is different to the claims that were once made.

In the great scheme of things, Brexit is of minor significance, but climate change is a different matter. If the political debate on climate change is characterized by the types of shenanigans employed during the Brexit process, then there is little hope that the electorate will be able to make well-informed decisions. The root of the problem is that politicians are more likely to be elected if they tell people what they want to hear, rather than paint a picture of reality and describe the hard choices that need to be made. This means that many political processes are characterized by hyperbolae and rhetoric rather a detailed assessment of the challenges we face.

The power of populism over pragmatism was illustrated in the US when Donald Trump was elected with a slogan of *Make America Great Again*. Trump offered a vision for America that was based on deregulation, tax cuts and protecting American jobs. It is unsurprising that voters were attracted by a message that claimed to offer simple solutions and promises of a better life.

Building support for a sustainable future requires the ability to present an alternative vision for society. Such a future vision must be not only be desirable but also credible. This new vision cannot be imposed by some self-nominated group but will need to evolve through a collective, social process. In effect, it will require an informed, democratic process that is untainted by spurious facts, manipulated by the media or the manoeuvrings of political parties in pursuit of self-interest.

Defining a vision for the future is only the first step. Fulfilling that vision will require the capabilities to manage a process of transition on a scale that has not been seen before. This process of transition will challenge our current beliefs and values. For example, do we believe that corporations have the right to make profit through activities that cause permanent damage to the environment? Do we want a financial system that increasingly concentrates wealth and power in the hands of a few? Do we believe that the current generation has the right to destroy the environment and leave the next generation to sort out the problems?

The rapid advancements in technology over the last 100 years might be claimed to result from factors such as the profit motive, free-market forces, commercial competition and corporate power that ensures the survival of the fittest. Yet, this free-market approach is not the only route to social, economic and technological innovation. Much of human advancement has resulted from collaboration, altruism and innate creative genius. The challenge for future societies will be to combine collaborative behaviours with the principles that encourage innovation and enterprise. Self-interest needs to be replaced by values that align personal aspirations with the wider aspects of societal well-being.

The process of transition

Any vision for the future needs to be rooted in reality. This means that it will need to explain how the transition to a sustainable society will be achieved. There is much that needs to change and any transition to a sustainable future must consider not just the technological and economic vision for the future but also what sort of society we are evolving into. In particular, it needs to offer reassurance that the journey to a sustainable future will not require sacrifices from some, while others gain significant advantages. In simple terms, we can identify three basic conditions that should guide the transition to a sustainable future:

- Not worse off.
- Preferably better off.
- A just transition.

There is one caveat worth mentioning in relation to the first point, *not worse off*. This needs to be measured against what would happen if we *don't* change compared with what would happen if we *do* change. Many nations, organizations and communities might feel perfectly happy with how things are at present, however, the current social and economic conditions cannot continue to offer a high standard of living to a large proportion of people in the developed world. The current trajectory will see greater pressure on limited resources and this will mean that an ever-smaller proportion of people will be able to enjoy a good quality of life.

The challenge is to ensure that the process of change is managed in ways that achieve an equitable social and economic transition – a *just transition*. Therefore, the process of transition should be managed so that nations, organizations and communities are *not worse off*, compared to the future if the changes had not occurred. For example, the major oil and gas companies currently earn huge revenues, employ thousands of people and provide good returns to their shareholders. However, the oil companies have recognized that this business model cannot continue. They do not have the option of continuing with business as usual, so they have to change and evolve. Many of these companies are developing alternative strategies that focus on the generation and supply of renewable energy. It might be that, in the future, their turnover might be lower, they might employ fewer people and their market dominance might be lower, but the point is that they will still be better off than if they *hadn't* changed their business model.

Expectations and the reality gap

In the developed world, particularly Western cultures, there is a sense that we are entitled to well-paid jobs, cheap consumer goods and opportunities for self-gratification. This expectation for a life of wealth and comfort took hold in the 1950s when there was high employment, unprecedented growth in material possessions and a sense that the human race was controller of all it surveyed. However, the reality for many people in the early part of the 21st century is that their lives are difficult, with little prospect of improvement. An increasingly large proportion of people struggle to meet the essential costs of living and see few chances to achieve a better life for themselves or their children. For the vast majority of people, expectations of a positive future are dwindling fast and there is a growing sense of injustice as people see an increasing gap between a small, wealthy elite and the vast majority of the population.

This disparity has been tolerated in part because many people felt unable to challenge it but also because the cultural values of a free-market economy offer the hope that everyone has the opportunity to *do well and get on in life*. Concepts such as the *American dream* encourage people to work hard so that they can become part of a glamorous, wealthy elite. However, in much of the developed world, the principles that underpin this aspirational economic model have become distorted and there is no longer such faith that hard work will be rewarded.

Growing inequality

Wealth and power are increasingly intertwined. Wealth not only brings commercial power but it also buys political influence. In the US, political lobbying and the funding of candidates, enables corporates to promote their interests. Concerns that corporations, foreign interests and unaccountable funds would have greater influence on US elections were expressed by President Obama in his State of the Union address, 2010.[2]

> Last week, the Supreme Court reversed a century of law that I believe will open the floodgates for special interests – including foreign corporations – to spend without limit in our elections. I don't think American elections should be bankrolled by America's most powerful interests, or worse, by foreign entities. They should be decided by the American people. And I'd urge Democrats and Republicans to pass a bill that helps correct some of these problems.'

Political parties of all colours will always seek to raise money, but the growing concentration of wealth in an increasingly small proportion of the population raises the risk that the wealthy and powerful will exert increasing influence over political decisions. An article in *The Guardian* newspaper, October 2015, highlighted the growing wealth gap: 'A report by Credit Suisse found that the world's richest 1% people have seen their share of the globe's total wealth increase from 42.5% at the height of the 2008 financial crisis to 50.1% in 2017, or $140tn.'[3]

This increasing disparity between the wealthy and the rest of society is not an inevitable consequence of a market economy. A market economy can be a highly effective way of allocating resources, distributing wealth and encouraging innovation. When a free-market economy operates under ethical principles, it can be an effective way of allocating wealth and rewarding effort. However, since the late 1970s, aggressive free-market political ideologies, such as neoliberalism, laissez-faire economics, the alt-right, have shaped the principles and mechanisms that determine how our economies operate, and there has been a drive towards personal and corporate self-interest rather than a belief in social cohesion and the common good. The result of this is that there has been an increasing concentration of wealth in an ever-smaller proportion of the population. This tiny segment of the population has acquired unparalleled levels of wealth, although the supporters of this ideology would probably claim that such wealth is justified and brings benefits to the wider population.

Success has been judged based on growth in GDP, which considers aggregate wealth, rather than seeking to understand how wealth is benefiting individuals within society. Falling levels of unemployment are hailed as a success, yet there is little visibility of the reality behind the statistics. Someone that had previously enjoyed a secure, well-paid job may, 20 years later, have two part-time jobs that are poorly paid and which offer no contract of employment or security. Indeed, there are many within society who work long hours, do difficult or exhausting jobs and yet still fail to earn enough to meet the basic costs of living.

Maybe we should not be surprised that politicians are reluctant to acknowledge these failings within the current economic system. After all, we would hardly expect a politician to say that GDP is increasing and unemployment is low but that many people are worse off. Even when it is self-evident that poverty, inequality and lack of opportunity blight many lives, there are many people who continue to proclaim the successes of the system.

The principles of a free-market economy are rooted in the idea that *profit is the reward for risk*. The flaws in this argument are, firstly, that markets are rarely *free*, and secondly, those that hold power and influence are in a position to arrange things so that they make high profits *without* significant risk. Profits are frequently the result of the ability to influence some aspect of the market, whether this is achieved through market dominance, preferential access to key decision makers or some other advantage. To an extent, these things will always exist; there will always be someone, who knows someone, who can help someone. Most businesses will have connections or market insight that gives them a commercial advantage. The problem is that we are moving to a position where a handful of organizations are now able to dominate markets at a global level.

The concern with this growing concentration of power, influence and wealth is that these vested interests not only distort the markets that they operate in but they also gain significant control of the political process, both nationally and internationally. As a result, they are able to use their political influence to protect an economic model that generates wealth through exploitation of the earth's resources with little accountability for the environmental consequences. Therefore, the causes of climate change will not be addressed until political processes are independent of the power and influence of interests that generate their wealth through the destruction of the environment.

The mechanisms to resist this concentration of power and influence may be imperfect, but they already exist; we have laws and regulations designed to prevent activities such as insider trading, bribery, corruption, money laundering, tax evasion and the misuse of power. What seems to be lacking is the political will to ensure greater transparency and ultimately, the prosecution of those that are guilty.

There needs to be both political change and corporate change. Political change will require evidence-based social, environmental and economic policies. Corporate change will require business strategies that are driven by environmental and social objectives, not profit maximization. Undoubtedly, there will be those who regard this proposal as an anathema to the principles of a free-market economy, but profit and purpose are not mutually exclusive, indeed, many well-respected voices from the corporate world have been advocating these principles. An online article by Steve Denning in *Forbes* provides a concise summary of the proposition.[4] It refers to a report by Nicole Notat and Jean Dominique Senard that was submitted to three French Government Ministries: Economy and Finance, Justice and Ecological Transition. To quote sections from the article by Steve Denning:

> The report condemns the goal as encouraging excessive financialization of the economy and a short-term perspective in the management of enterprises. Their principal recommendation to deal with the issue is to require corporations to specify their 'raison

d'être' or 'reason for being' and base the enterprise's governance on that concept.

The full report begins with a quote from Peter Drucker: 'Profit is not an end in itself' for the company. It notes that 'these words are not those of a political manifesto, but of the American Peter F. Drucker, one of the inventors of modern management. He argues that 'Profitability is not the purpose of the business but a limiting factor. Profit is neither the explanation nor the cause nor the motive of decisions and behavior in business, but the testing of their validity.' (Steve Denning in *Forbes*, 13 May 2018)

The current political process is failing

We are in a situation that is characterized by commercial organizations driven by profit, political policies influenced by vested interests and political processes that are failing to resolve the incompatibility of our current economic model with a sustainable society. Part of the problem is that we are pursuing the wrong goals and using the wrong measures of success. For example, governments are focused on GDP in the way that organizations are focused on profit. Business measures such as profit, turnover and market share tell us nothing about the value an organization has added to society. High-level national indicators such as GDP, economic growth or levels of employment tell us little about the reality of life for individuals, communities, societal well-being or the state of the planet.

The consequence of pursuing inappropriate goals is that governments adopt inappropriate policies. For example, since the financial crash in 2008 many countries adopted policies that reduced expenditure on public services. This age of austerity has been characterized by the poor and vulnerable being denied essential services while the profits of the major corporates have increased. Unless we change the measures that governments use to assess the success of their political policies, we will not have visibility of the problems that confront us.

The analogy of the global financial crash

The current problems faced by our economies are, in part, a consequence of the 2008 global financial crash. This event symbolized the weakness of a financial system that fuelled consumption through credit. Governments were complicit in this process as it boosted short-term economic growth. One would have hoped that regulations and policies would have been in place to prevent a catastrophic financial collapse, but governments failed to act and, instead, watched the global economy drive off the edge of a cliff. The 2008 financial collapse offers a worrying analogy for environmental collapse:

- The risks associated with an unregulated financial system were frequently expressed.
- Governments, business and banks were reluctant to introduce financial controls that might hamper growth and wealth.
- Individuals that raised concerns were often ignored or vilified.

The 2008 financial crash caused significant disruption to the world economy; however, ten years later most economies are now back to business as usual. By a mixture of luck and judgement, plus massive injections of financial support, governments managed to prop up the financial institutions and save many of the major corporations that teetered on the brink of collapse. Yet, at the time of writing, just over ten years later, the level of personal debt in many advanced economies is higher now than it was in 2008. Once again, we stand on the edge of the financial abyss.

If there is one sign of hope from 2008 it is the fact that survival and self-interest can have a powerful effect on mobilizing resources when a crisis happens. When the global crash occurred, it was amazing how quickly national resources were diverted to address the problem, illustrating what is possible when political leaders decide to take action. Following the economic crash, there was a happy convergence of the interests of the super-wealthy, global political leaders, major corporations and the financial institutions.

Unfortunately, addressing climate change does not benefit from the same happy convergence of interests. Indeed, many sources of wealth may be threatened if we move away from our current global economic model. A transition from fossil fuels will dramatically affect the wealth of national economies in regions such as the Middle East, US, Russia, South America and parts of North Africa. The beef industry and animal agriculture is a significant contributor to greenhouse gases; it causes pollution of rivers and drives demand for land in areas such as the Amazon rain forest. Yet the beef industry is a major contributor to many economies. As a result, governments and corporate interests are resistant to challenges that might be levelled at it. There is a recurring theme that governments are resistant to changes that disrupt the interests of certain sectors of the economy.

A hard change is going to come

At present, the consequences of climate change are, for many people, fairly minor and secondary to the daily struggle of everyday life, however, there will soon come a point when a large proportion of the global population sees a direct relationship between climate change and a growing threat to them and their families. When this happens, the usual political platitudes of *better times ahead* will no longer be credible, and confidence in the current socio-economic model will crumble.

The coming decade will see a growing number of extreme events such as floods, drought, the collapse of natural habitats, forest fires and other devastating consequences of climate change. These events will result in huge numbers of people being displaced, unprecedented migration and increased risks of regional and international conflict. If we are lucky, there may still be time for political and corporate leaders to take action. If we are unlucky, there will be a desperate struggle for personal and political advantage as conflicting groups seek to protect their stake in diminishing resources. If this happens, the poor and disenfranchised will be the first to suffer, but ultimately large proportions of global society will suffer. Protests and civil unrest will follow, and this anger will provide a platform for the emergence of alternative political models and will open the door to demagogues promising simplistic solutions to complex problems. History does not offer much reassurance that such a scenario will lead to a better society.

As global threats increase, we will have to decide whether our survival strategies are based on competition or collaboration. Much of our economic and political thinking is premised on the concept of *survival of the fittest*. This thinking is rooted in Darwinian theories of evolution, but this was an over-simplified view of how species evolved. Recent thinking, exemplified by Willis Harman and Elisabet Sahtouris[5] proposes that successful organisms, ecosystems and societies succeed through their ability to coexist, rather than through their ability to destroy the opposition. Similarly, human civilization and the survival of the planet are likely to depend on beliefs, values and attitudes that result in behaviours that seek collaboration and shared interests.

Moving towards a sustainable future

Our political and corporate leaders not only need the capability to define a future vision, but they also need the capability to deliver that vision. Translating vision into reality requires the ability to manage a range of factors that enable a successful transition from *where we are now* to *where do we want to be*. The following list, while not pretending to be comprehensive, illustrates the diversity of factors that need to be managed.

Goals

A vision is aspirational, while goals imply commitment, and goals should define the outcomes that are required. For example, one high-level goal would be to achieve net zero emissions of greenhouse gases by 2050. Such high-level goals may be supported by more detailed goals. For example, the next level of detail might include goals relating to specific greenhouse gases: CO_2, methane, refrigerants and so forth.

Other high-level goals are likely to relate to issues such as rain forests, oceans and rivers, buildings and cities, land use and food production. Clearly, these goals are focused on addressing climate change, but the vision for a future society will require goals that relate to the sort of sustainable society that we want to live in: equality of opportunity, the distribution of wealth, international collaboration and so forth.

Targets

Each goal will have a target, or set of targets. For example, CO_2 emissions from vehicles might currently account for approximately 20 per cent of all CO_2. The targets might be to reduce current levels by 10 per cent in three years, 25 per cent in five years, 75 per cent in ten years and so on. Similarly, the proportion of energy produced by renewables will have targets. For example, 60 per cent of energy to be produced by renewables by 2030 and 95 per cent by 2040.

Plan

It might seem obvious, but any major programme being delivered by government will need a plan that sets out major milestones, key activities, timescales, resources and costings. Such plans should be developed through consultation with stakeholders, and should be widely understood and available for scrutiny by the wider public.

Drivers

The ability to achieve the various targets depends on an understanding of the drivers that affect whether the target will, or will not, be achieved. For example, one of the key factors to drive the switch from petrol/diesel to electric cars is likely to be the comparable costs of different types of vehicle. Similarly, one of the drivers affecting the switch to renewable energy will be relative cost per kilowatt-hour. Understanding these drivers means that we know how to influence the behaviours that determine the progress towards the intended outcome.

Visibility

Clearly, it is essential that we have visibility of the progress being made against intended targets. This will enable progress to be monitored, corrective action to be taken and will help validate the assumed linkage between the drivers and targets. Visibility enables different groups to see and understand the changes that are occurring. The value of this visibility is that it allows outcomes to be reviewed and corrective actions taken.

Regulation

The actions of consumers and businesses are strongly influenced by factors such as regulation, legislation and taxation. For example, regulations that require manufacturers to phase out production of petrol/diesel vehicles by 2035 will have a direct impact on vehicle emissions. Legislation that requires all plastic packaging to be biodegradable will reduce the damage caused by plastics in the environment.

Enforcement

The ability to enforce regulation is essential. Relevant organizations will need the capability to monitor all activities that fall within their remit. Where they identify breaches of regulation, they will need the authority to take action against offenders. For example, there is little benefit in having regulations relating to the discharge of pollutants into rivers unless there is the capability to enforce breaches of such regulation.

Mandate

Governments are rarely in a position where they can impose regulation without some level of support from the electorate. For example, society broadly accepts that taxation is necessary to enable public goods and services to be provided. This broad understanding provides a mandate for imposing regulations and enforcing them. This mandate is dependent upon a belief within the electorate that government, and the individual politicians that compose the government, have the integrity and competence to define regulations that are in the interests of society as a whole. If there is a sense that the government are under the influence of vested interests or pursuing actions without due regard for the wider benefit of society, then the mandate evaporates.

Norms

The term *cultural norms* refers to the beliefs, values, attitudes and behaviours that exist within society. Inevitably, there will be variances within society and the greater the level of divergence, the more difficult it will be to achieve consensus on the factors discussed above. Achieving a transition within society will be problematic if the cultural norms do not inherently support the vision that is being proposed. For example, some groups within society may have little understanding of the threat from climate change and seek to resist any action that is perceived as changing their current way of life.

As well as identifying the types of activity that need to be managed by governments, it is also worth considering some of the factors that might lie outside the direct control of the government but which will affect the outcome. Again, this is not intended as an exhaustive list, but rather it is intended to show the type of issues that need to be considered. Examples might include:

• The degree to which the electorate are informed and engaged.
• The level of transparency in the way political decisions are made.
• The ability of a politically neutral civil service to undertake its duties.
• The degree to which government policies are guided by trustworthy evidence.
• The effectiveness and motivation of opposition parties.
• The integrity and clarity of information provided to the electorate.

- The influence of vested interests such as corporates, wealthy/ powerful individuals and pressure groups.
- The level of trust that exists with other international governments.

It is worth expanding on a few of these points:

The degree to which the electorate are informed and engaged

If the electorate is largely ignorant of the implications of government actions (or the motivations behind such actions), then it becomes far easier for government to pursue a specific political agenda with minimal resistance. Similarly, a government that is incompetent will find it easier to avoid criticism if the electorate take little interest in politics or are easily fobbed-off with simplistic explanations. An uninformed electorate will be susceptible to *sound-bite politics* and easily convinced by charismatic leaders. When the electorate have little ability to assess the validity of the claims being made by government, or have little understanding of the complexity behind difficult issues then, inevitably, voters will rely on gut instinct to guide their support for a particular leader or party. Similarly, patriotism or religion can be a positive and unifying force within societies that are informed and politically engaged, but where the electorate has little understanding of economic, social or international issues then patriotism becomes a powerful force with which to influence opinion.

The level of transparency in the way political decisions are made

Government policy is likely to be influenced and informed by a wide range of ideas, opinions and individuals. Diversity of views is probably going to lead to better policies and more representative government. It is difficult to prescribe the process by which government should seek to obtain such views but it is important that there is transparency of where the views originate, who is promoting them and what their motivations might be. If policymaking is influenced by secretive cabals, attempting to sidestep the required democratic processes or operating without proper transparency, then the process of democratic government is undermined.

The ability of a politically neutral civil service to undertake its duties

Good government will be best achieved when it is provided with good quality advice. The role of the civil service is critical and it is important that senior civil servants have the freedom to assess evidence impartially, rather than be required to provide information that fits the intended views of their political masters.

The degree to which government policies are guided by trustworthy evidence

If we are to address the problems facing society and the future of the planet, it is essential that politicians make decisions that are based on independent and trustworthy evidence. Such evidence needs to be researched and assessed by suitably qualified bodies. We need to avoid situations where dubious or carefully selected evidence is used to justify intended policy. In times of crisis, it is particularly important that the electorate should have confidence that the relevant issues are understood, the options are evaluated by suitably qualified experts and the information is presented to government in a fair and balanced manner. This process should be auditable and transparent. While government would be the final arbiters on the decisions taken, the electorate should have confidence in the evidence presented to government and how it was evaluated.

The effectiveness and motivation of opposition parties

The primary role of the political opposition is to hold the incumbent party to account. This has the advantage that a balancing force is continually questioning the competence of the party in power, but the weakness of this process is the risk that opposition parties focus on the things that the electorate want to hear, rather than raise difficult issues, such as climate change. Any political party that seeks to raise contentious and poorly understood issues, risks isolating themselves from the electorate. This means that opposition parties may focus more on riding the wave of public opinion, rather than raising issues that might be difficult or contentious.

The integrity and clarity of information provided to the electorate

Political campaigns appear increasingly characterized by dubious claims and unsubstantiated allegations. In particular, the process of political campaigning relies heavily on social media to target specific audience groups with messages that address their individual concerns. There are growing concerns that well-financed groups are able to influence the political process by funding intensive social media campaigns, while seeking to protect their anonymity. An open, democratic process requires transparency of the source of funds for political campaigns.

The influence of vested interests: corporates, wealthy/powerful individuals and pressure groups

Governments, and potential parties of government, seek to build and consolidate their power. Inevitably, this requires money and support from those with influence. Where governments are indebted to wealthy individuals or corporates we should not be surprised when governments act to support the interests of their primary supporters. The less transparency there is, the greater the opportunities for the political system to serve these vested interests.

The level of trust that exists with other international governments

The big issues of our time, such as climate change, the global economy, international conflict and pandemics, require international cooperation. Governments that do not have the trust of other nations will find themselves ostracized and isolated.

This list of issues is not definitive, but it does suggest some ideas for evaluating political parties and the broader political process.

The scientific evidence is clear; we have to dramatically reduce greenhouse gas emissions in the next decade and become net zero by 2050, at the absolute latest and preferably by 2040. To achieve this, governments and organizations will need the capabilities necessary to manage fundamental changes within our economies, societies and the culture that underpins how we live our lives. By evaluating the governments, corporations and the intergovernmental organizations that are tasked with coordinating international action, we might gain some insight as to whether they are likely to succeed or whether the political processes lack the characteristics necessary to enable change to happen.

5

Effective Government Intervention

Chapter summary

The key theme of this chapter is that government intervention is essential as market forces alone will not deliver the changes required within the timescales necessary. It explores the relationship between government policies and the various interdependencies that determine whether such policies will be effective. One of the propositions of this chapter is that simply designing policies is not sufficient. Successful government intervention requires an understanding of the factors that determine whether the policies will achieve their intended outcomes.

Introduction

Climate change will, in time, affect everyone, but at the present time there is a pervading sense of, *it's not really going to affect me.* As a consequence, governments face little pressure from the electorate. Significant pressure on governments to address climate change will only occur when the majority of people see a direct and probably imminent consequence for their lives. Currently, there seems to be a general awareness that climate change is a potential problem, but there is not a sense that there is an imminent threat to civilization. At present, the direct impact of climate change only threatens a relatively small proportion of the global population, primarily those in the emerging economies. Many within the advanced economies are still isolated from the immediate consequences of climate change, although this is starting to change as we see increasing incidents of forest fires, floods and extreme weather affecting the wealthier parts of the world.

Populations within the less developed countries, particularly those at subsistence levels, are more likely to be affected by climate change as even slight variations in weather patterns can disrupt those living at subsistence levels. However, these populations rarely have a strong political voice, and pressure for change may ultimately require voters in countries with advanced economies to be directly affected by the consequences of climate change. At some point in the near future, climate change will affect those economies that had so far escaped the direct consequences. Climate change will become the overwhelming priority of governments and there will be a realization that all nations have to take action and unite in a common goal of reversing climate change.

National governments are very effective at collaborating, and the concept of *shared goals* across the international community already exists; it is called global trade. The shared goals of wealth generation, profit maximization and, hopefully, a sense of social responsibility guide the actions of governments and business. The problem is that our model for the free market is premised on the idea that profit maximization is the primary goal. If we can shift this concept to a position where profit takes account of environmental costs, then we have the basis for a sustainable free-market economy. We need to build on the strengths of the free-market economy while creating frameworks that enable it to operate in ways that value the natural environment. Market forces are highly effective at allocating resources to activities that create the most value and we need to harness these same market forces to guide changes in the market: the shift to low emission vehicles, the switch to renewables and the adoption of the circular economy. The challenge is to ensure that environmental costs are accounted for.

The other change that will be required is an acknowledgement that governments have an essential part to play in driving the social and economic changes required. While we need to harness the strength of market forces, we cannot abdicate responsibility to the market.

The need for government intervention

While writing this book I attended a number of meetings held at the Houses of Parliament where politicians, business leaders and technical experts presented proposals relating to future energy policy. These events focused on future energy strategy and a recurring theme appeared to be that the government would outline the strategy, but organizations were expected to deliver the changes. There is a logic to this approach, but it does require government to do more than set aspirational goals and targets. Some level of intervention will be required.

At one of these events, I asked about government intervention and the extent to which this would be used to encourage the process of transition. The response was that the free market would lead to the best outcomes. This apparent reluctance to intervene on the basis that it would distort market forces was surprising as the UK is a mixed economy where it is largely accepted that there are areas where government intervention is required. The challenge for the transition to a sustainable economy rests on the issues the politicians believe require government intervention. If government ministers believe that intervention is unnecessary in the energy sector then the market will determine the pace of change and this will favour commercial strategies that maximize the return on investment from existing technologies.

Government intervention will be required to influence a wide range of factors that determine future energy, for example deployment of technologies such as smart grids, coordination to ensure interoperability between systems, agreement on standards and regulations. The government also has an important role in influencing buyer behaviour. For example, incentives to encourage households to install solar panels, taxes on petrol/diesel to encourage consumers to switch to fuel-efficient vehicles and grants to encourage building insulation. Government intervention will be essential but this is only one element within a number of factors that need to be addressed. These factors can be categorized as follows.

Enablers

This refers to those activities that help define the vision, goals and targets. It also includes the organizations that initiate and enable the process of change. For example:

- Government departments.
- Watchdog organizations.
- Banks.
- Universities.
- Pressure groups.
- Industry sector bodies.

Drivers

This refers to those factors that influence economic and social activity. Examples include:

- Policies.
- Education.
- Media.
- Financial.
- Legal.
- Regulations.
- Guidelines.

Behaviours

This refers to the actions of individuals, communities and organizations. Behaviours will be strongly influenced by the *drivers*, such as government policies, regulations and so forth, but they will also be influenced by beliefs, values and attitudes. Beliefs can be deeply engrained, but values and attitudes are more malleable, especially under the influence of peer pressure or charismatic leadership. For example, driving an expensive car may be seen as an important status symbol, and behaviours are reflected in the way that:

- We live our lives.
- Society operates.
- Organizations provide goods and services.

Outcomes

This refers to the changes that are achieved. In the case of climate change, the desired outcomes might be to:

- Reduce greenhouse gas emissions.
- Protect and restore the rain forests.
- Protect the fertility of agricultural land.

The relationship between these factors is illustrated in Figure 5.1. Figure 5.1 seeks to illustrate the multitude of interdependencies that will determine the effectiveness of government action to create a more sustainable society. For the purpose of neatness, Figure 5.1 shows the different categories in separate columns, with a sequential flow from one column to the next, categorized as *enablers*, *drivers* and *behaviour change*. In reality, there is no such neatness to these relationships. Each item interconnects with multiple others and there will be feedback connections that are difficult to represent in a single figure. However, the key message of Figure 5.1 is that a strategy for a sustainable future will require a holistic approach that seeks to understand the whole system, rather than isolated policies to address specific parts of the system.

Achieving a transition to a sustainable global society will require us to rethink the nature of society, social purpose and our relationship with the natural environment. Political leaders and the international community will need to move away from goals such as economic growth, and set objectives that are consistent with a sustainable global economy. However, it is unlikely that there will be complete agreement on what the new global society will look like. Therefore, there will need to be flexibility to allow different national governments and geopolitical regions to adopt a variety of socio-economic models. For example, the US may have a different vision for a future socio-economic model than China or Europe. However, there will need to be agreement on core objectives, such as the elimination of carbon emissions, preventing destruction of rain forests and controls on the exploitation of natural resources.

In the UK, we have a relatively good track record of changing consumer behaviour to reduce environmental damage. Examples

Figure 5.1: Factors that determine outcomes

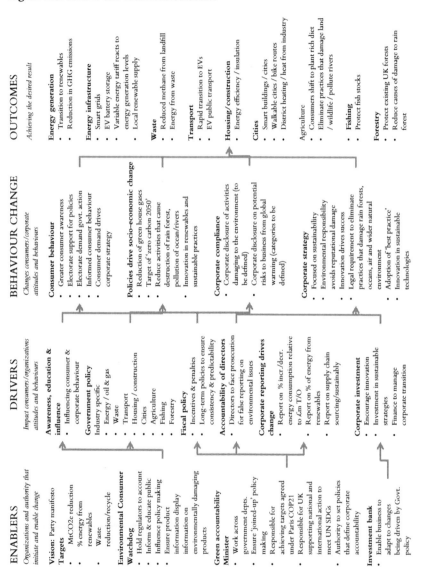

Source: Richard Joy

include the adoption of fuel-efficient cars, influenced by high fuel taxes and concessions on road tax for low emission vehicles and significant reductions in waste sent to landfill, helped by introducing effective recycling schemes and a reduction in the consumption of plastic bags. These examples of changes in consumer behaviour have been achieved because the aims are understood and broadly supported. However, these are examples of single-issue changes, with a clear linkage between the action taken by government (make consumers pay for each carrier bag) and the intended outcome (reduce plastic waste). Building support for changes that will affect all aspects of social and economic activity, such as becoming net zero, is far more complex than addressing a single issue and will require governments to address five key areas.

1. Goals and strategies

Governments need to set out clear goals and strategies. The reasons need to be explained and the outcomes need to be supported.

2. Success criteria

Governments need to establish new measures of success. This means moving away from measures such as economic growth and GDP, and adopting alternative measures such as environmental impact, social fairness and well-being.

3. New economic model

There needs to be a clear rationale for a new economic model and this needs to be supported by governments at a national and international level.

4. Values, attitudes and behaviours

Cultural norms need to evolve, particularly in the wealthy industrialized economies, so that high consumption of non-renewable resources is seen as undesirable and socially unacceptable.

5. New skills and capabilities

The current global economy is built on cheap energy resources. We need to anticipate the impending decline in these resources and establish patterns of economic activity that will achieve sustainable development. This will create demand for new skills and jobs.

Change is inevitable

Even those who deny climate change cannot dispute that fossil fuels are a finite resource. While it is true that there are huge untapped reserves of hydrocarbons, the cost of extraction rises as the process of exploration and production becomes increasingly complex. As a consequence, the profit margins in the oil and gas sector are declining and the profit margins in renewables are becoming more attractive. As regions scale-up their renewable capacity, the cost of production falls, further increasing the gulf between fossil fuels and renewables.

The decline of the oil and gas sector looks increasingly inevitable. This will have serious economic consequences for the oil producing economies and this, in turn, will have geopolitical consequences. The potential for social unrest and political instability in regions such as the Middle East, South America and Russia are not difficult to imagine. The geopolitical consequences of transitioning to a net zero global economy need to be anticipated and managed.

The shift away from fossil fuels is inevitable but we cannot wait for market forces to manage this change. The oil industry has invested in assets that have a long payback period, and it will want to secure a return on these assets for some considerable period to come. The problem is that climate change will pass the tipping point long before the oil industry has achieved its desired return on investment. International intervention will be required to support the transition of economies that currently depend on fossil fuels.

Prevarication is not an option

We know that radical social and economic change is possible, particularly in times of major crisis, such as war or a global pandemic, when society understands the reasons for disruption. The question is *How bad does it have to get before societies demand action?*

Social groups can be remarkably poor at recognizing and responding to external threats. Why, for example, did the population of Pompeii fail to move away from the volcano when it first started to erupt? It is believed that there was 12 hours of volcanic activity and falling ash before the major eruption and consequential pyroclastic flows (super-heated air) killed the surrounding population. Why didn't people try to escape during that 12-hour period?

There is a sense that we are in a similar situation to the citizens of Pompeii; we have evidence that climate change is happening, but we prefer to ignore the impending catastrophe. There may be various reasons why people prefer to believe that climate change is not a significant threat. Some of these reasons relate to disinformation and a deliberate strategy of casting doubt on the scientific evidence. Other reasons might relate to a human characteristic to avoid 'over-reacting'. Psychological experiments have shown that people prefer to remain in a *known* environment, even if it is dangerous, rather than move to an *unknown* environment that would be safer.[1] These two factors, the existence of doubt and a preference for hoping for the best, mean that it is difficult to mobilize public action until the crisis is imminent.

We cannot wait for market forces to lead the way to a sustainable economy or for communities to initiate the actions that are required. These factors will be important, but on their own they will not be sufficient. Radical social and economic change will require government intervention. Whether this is a series of reactive events or a coordinated strategy to move towards a sustainable society remains to be seen.

6

The Energy Transition

Chapter summary

This chapter examines the rate at which carbon is being emitted into the atmosphere and looks at the concept of the carbon budget. It examines the policy gap that exists between the projected reduction in carbon emissions resulting from current policies, and the required reduction in carbon emissions. It examines the consequences of a failure to reduce carbon emissions rapidly and how this will require a cliff edge reduction in emissions, or risk reaching the tipping point. It also offers a summary of key data to illustrate the scale of the energy transition that is required.

The scale of the threat

Most governments acknowledge the threat of climate change and have plans to reduce carbon emissions over the next few decades. Although some governments are only making slow progress, others are working hard to become more sustainable. One of the success stories is the UK, which has achieved a significant shift towards renewables, and these efforts deserve recognition.

The UK is ranked as one of the best performing nations in reducing CO_2. This is an important achievement but, as always, it is important to understand the full picture. Part of this success is due to the increasing proportion of energy that is provided by renewables, but it is also a result of the switch away from industrial production in areas such as steel, concrete, industrial chemicals and manufacturing. The UK economy is increasingly based on service industries and relies on importing the industrial products that it needs. This means that the UK exports its carbon emissions to those countries that produce the manufactured goods.

Even if we ignore the impact of exporting carbon emissions, the next question is: *Is the UK on track to deliver its carbon reduction targets by 2050?* To answer this question, we need to understand the target set by the government and to look at the policies that are being developed to meet these targets.

UK government emissions target

The UK government passed the Climate Change Act in 2008, which set a target to reduce emissions to 80 per cent of 1990 emission levels by 2050. Ideally, the target should be to reduce carbon emissions so that the economy is net-zero by 2050. However, this has huge implications across industry sectors and following table illustrates one scenario for reducing emissions across the sectors that are the major source of greenhouse gas emissions.

Table 6.1: Carbon reduction targets to achieve net zero by 2050

Sector	2016 $MtCO_2e$	2020 $MtCO_2e$	% decline
Power	79	3	96%
Heat	89	4	95%
Transport	121	5	91%
Industry	100	32	68%
Agriculture	84	47	44%
TOTAL	**473**	**91**	80%

Note: $MtCO_2e$ = Million metric tonnes, CO_2 equivalent

Source: Data reproduced from a report produced for the Liberal Democrats by Culmer Raphael and Iken Associates. This report was commissioned by the Liberal Democrats in order to assess the policy implications associated with transitioning to a net-zero economy. The report was produced by Culmer Raphael and Iken Associates.

This shows that some sectors of the economy are projected to achieve radical reductions, such as energy, heat and transport, but other sectors will struggle to reduce emissions by more than about 50 per cent, such as industry and agriculture. This will mean that either the carbon emissions need to be prevented from entering the atmosphere by some form of technology at the point of release into the atmosphere, or the emissions have to be offset by actions such as planting trees. Although carbon offset strategies offer a mechanism to fund environmental restorative activities, ultimately we should aim to stop pumping carbon into the atmosphere *and* restore the natural environment. However, the good news is that some sectors of the economy are capable of radically reducing carbon emissions with the technologies that are now available.

UK government policies

Policies will be required to achieve these targets, but an assessment by the Department for Business, Energy and Industrial Strategy (BEIS) suggests that there is a *policy gap* between the required level of CO_2 reduction and the projected level of reduction, based on current policies.[1]

Figure 6.1 illustrates the anticipated impact of current policies (the grey shaded area) in reducing carbon emissions and shows that current policies will not achieve the required reduction (the dotted line).

Figure 6.1: UK Government emission target policy gap

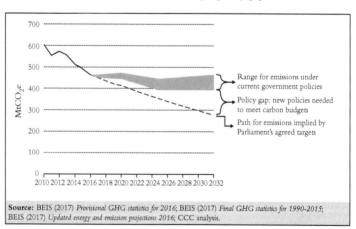

Source: Climate Change Committee (2017) *Meeting Carbon Budgets: Closing the Policy Gap. 2017 Report to Parliament.*[2]

The above information relates specifically to the UK and it would be interesting to see the equivalent figures for other nations and to map the aggregated results against global reduction targets. The scale of the *policy gap* would probably be depressingly large.

But, even if all countries that signed up to the Paris Agreement successfully implemented policies to achieve their targets to reduce emissions it is questionable whether this would be sufficient to prevent global temperatures breaching the 1.5°C limit.

Current prospects look bleak

If we take immediate action to switch to low carbon technologies, we might be able to buy ourselves time to avoid passing the tipping point. However, the longer we delay the more dramatic the rate of CO_2 reduction will need to be, and the risks will be greater.

Figure 6.2 illustrates how delaying the transition to zero-carbon energy sources will require more dramatic reductions in carbon emissions in the remaining years. If the current rate of greenhouse gas emissions continues through to 2025, we will

Figure 6.2: Carbon reduction scenarios

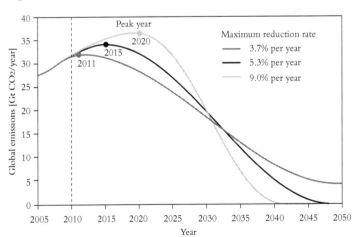

Source: WBGU – German Advisory Council on Global Change (2009) *World in Transition. A Social Contract for Sustainability. Flagship Report*, Berlin: WBGU.[3]

face a cliff edge reduction in CO_2 emissions in order to meet the 1.5°C limit; the longer we delay, the greater the scale of reduction that will be required.

Confusing and contradictory policies

At present, there appears to be broad support within the UK for government policies that encourage the switch to renewables. However, there is a confused logic behind government strategy as the level of subsidies to the oil industry is greater than those to renewables. An article in *The Guardian* (January 2019) reported on the findings of a report by the European Commission, that the UK had the biggest fuel subsidies in the EU: 'The UK leads the European Union in giving subsidies to fossil fuels, according to a report from the European commission. It found €12bn (£10.5bn) a year in support for fossil fuels in the UK, significantly more than the €8.3bn spent on renewable energy.' The article goes on to say: 'The total fossil fuel subsidies in the EU were €55bn in 2016, the report concluded. "This is a very high number, given we are reaching the deadline for some of their [phase out] promises," said Ipek Gencsu, subsidies expert at the Overseas Development Institute (ODI).'[4]

A separate article in *The Guardian* provides information for the US and globally:

> A report from Oil Change International (OCI) investigated American energy industry subsidies and found that in 2015–2016, the federal government provided $14.7bn per year to the oil, gas, and coal industries, on top of $5.8bn of state-level incentives (globally, the figure is around $500bn). And the report only accounted for production subsidies, excluding consumption subsidies (support to consumers to lower the cost of fossil fuel use – another $14.5bn annually) as well as the costs of carbon and other fossil fuel pollutants.[5]

It seems likely that subsidies to the fossil fuel industry will continue for some time. However, there is a contradiction in a political ideology that, on one hand, claims that free-market forces offer to allocate resources effectively, yet on the other hand, provide huge subsidies to support certain industry sectors. The justification for offering special treatment may be that the fossil fuel sector is intricately connected to our global economy and that the decline of this sector will damage our economic wealth. This is undoubtedly true as much of our current economic activity is dependent on fossil fuels; our manufacturing industries depend on plastics, our financial systems invest heavily in the sector and international relations are shaped by strategies to secure oil and gas. But this is not an argument for the continued destruction of the planet. Instead, it underpins the argument that governments need to fund the costs of transition. However, at present, the effect is to perpetuate an industry sector that is the primary cause of climate change.

The energy transition will not only require changes in the way that we produce energy but it will also require changes in the way that we distribute energy, store energy and price energy. All of these will require clear, government-led strategies to ensure that business has the confidence to make long-term investments and that appropriate standards are defined to ensure the compatibility of new technologies as they are developed. None of these things happen if government stand on the sidelines.

Future energy infrastructure will require smart grids that have the capability to manage changes between the demand and supply of energy, for example, by intelligent connections to battery capacity in EV, and manage real-time pricing that encourages consumers to adjust energy usage according to fluctuations in energy supply. The traditional national grid infrastructure that has been based on large power stations feeding power into a nationally distributed power distribution network will see dramatic changes. In particular, we will see growth in *pro-sumers* (households, businesses and local communities that both produce and consume electricity). This means that there will be greater reliance on multiple sources of renewable energy feeding into local and micro-grids.

One of the problems with renewables is that there are peaks and troughs in energy supply due to changes in wind or sun. Demand response technologies are developing rapidly and the next five to ten years will provide technologies that manage the problems of intermittent generation, such as energy stored in battery or kinetic energy systems.

Coal and gas-powered power stations will be phased out and the economics of nuclear power will change. The real cost of nuclear energy has been disguised by subsidies to offset the high cost of construction, operation and decommissioning. If the real cost were to be met by the consumer it would be unable to compete with renewables. The primary justification for including nuclear power within the energy mix is that it provides a reliable baseload. An article in *energypost.eu* offers a useful insight into the debate on the need for nuclear power.

> For example, the UK Energy Secretary Amber Rudd, attempted to justify the decision to build the proposed Hinkley Point C nuclear power station on the grounds that 'we have to secure baseload electricity.'
>
> Similarly, former Australian Industry Minister Ian Macfarlane recently claimed at a uranium industry conference: 'Baseload, zero emission, the only way it can be produced is by hydro or nuclear.'
>
> Underlying this claim are three key assumptions. First, that baseload power is actually a good and necessary thing. In fact, what it really means is too much power when you don't want it, and not enough when you do. What we need is flexible power (and flexible demand too) so that supply and demand can be matched instant by instant.
>
> The second assumption is that nuclear power is a reliable baseload supplier. In fact it's no such thing. All nuclear power stations are subject to tripping out for safety reasons or technical faults. That means that a 3.2GW nuclear power station has to be matched by 3.2GW of expensive 'spinning reserve' that can be called in at a moment's notice.
>
> The third is that the only way to supply baseload power is from baseload power stations, such as nuclear, coal and gas, designed to run flat-out all the time ...[6]

The rationale that underpinned energy policies 20 years ago no longer holds true. We need energy strategies that exploit the opportunities that are now available, rather than policies that are based on assumptions that applied to centralized national grids many years ago. Energy generation will move away from a system that relies on a relatively small number of large power stations responding to fluctuating demand, to a system with multiple sources of generation that feed intelligent grid systems and real-time balancing of demand through reactive pricing, coupled with high-capacity energy storage.

It will take time for energy infrastructure to develop this real-time, responsive capability. Similarly, it will be some years before we have energy storage systems that have the capacity to balance out the gaps between demand and supply. In addition, the demand for electricity is likely to increase dramatically as we switch from fossil fuels. Therefore, in the short-term, nuclear power will probably be required if we are to achieve net zero by 2050. The advantage of nuclear is that it offers resilience to an energy supply system that is not currently available with existing renewable technologies. However, nuclear power still has two major problems:

- It is expensive (when the real, full-life cost is accounted for).
- The waste products are highly dangerous and remain so for thousands of years.

Innovations offer the possibility of lowering the cost of nuclear power, (small modular reactors), but it is not clear how these potentially lower prices will compare to the costs of renewables. In addition, the risks associated with nuclear waste remain. It is important that the short-term role of nuclear power does not become confused with the long-term strategic goal of developing cheap, clean, green energy. Resources should not be diverted *away from* renewables in order to support nuclear. Instead, investment in nuclear offers an interim solution while we continue to expand renewables, develop intelligent grid systems and commercialize innovative energy storage technologies.

A future based on renewable energy is within touching distance and the last few years have seen significant progress in turning an aspiration into reality. Examples include:

- Denmark generated 47% of its power from renewables in 2019.[7]
- UK generated 42.9% of its electricity from renewables in 2020.[8]
- China generates nearly 40 per cent of its energy from renewables.[9]

The good news is that renewables are starting to offer a realistic alternative to fossil fuels. The bad news is that the total demand for energy is increasing, and about 40 per cent of new generating capacity is provided by fossil fuels, and we continue to build power stations that pump carbon into the atmosphere.

Growth in renewables

The technologies that generate energy from renewables are now well established. They have proven to be reliable, cost efficient and capable of operating in different conditions across the globe. Renewable technologies are being incorporated within national energy infrastructure and they account for about 60 per cent of the new capacity that is being built. However, this still means that 40 per cent of all new energy capacity is being produced by methods that produce greenhouse gas.

Renewable energy is one of the good news stories, but the scale of the task to replace fossil fuel energy should not be underestimated. The global demand for electricity continues to rise and this is set to increase dramatically as technologies such as EV become widely adopted. This additional demand must not be met by electricity generation that creates greenhouse gas. In 2019, fossil fuels accounted for approximately 84 per cent of global primary energy consumption. Therefore the energy supply industry not only has to meet 100 per cent of all additional demand from renewables, but it also has to replace over 80 per cent of the existing capacity.[10]

Wind and solar energy accounts for about 8 per cent of renewables. The majority of energy produced from renewables is from hydropower. One of the challenges facing hydropower schemes is that they can cause significant environmental, social and political consequences as many schemes involve building dams across major rivers. Such schemes are likely to disrupt water supplies to communities and nations that are downstream from the dam. Large areas of land might need to be flooded with consequent effects on livelihoods and the natural environment. Such events can cause social and political tensions and it should not be assumed that hydropower offers an easy option for further growth in renewable power. Another consideration in the debate on hydroelectric power is that many large dams are coming to the end of their safe life and will need to be replaced. The safe life is in the order of about 70 years. If dams fail, they can have a devastating impact on surrounding areas. In 1975 the Banqiao Dam in China burst, causing an estimated 150,000 deaths. Currently there are approximately 60,000 large dams around the world, which could have a devastating impact if they fail. Strategies to replace many of these dams will be required over the next couple of decades. The consequences of failure on the energy supply for these regions also needs to be considered.

Renewables as a share of final energy use

The three main uses for energy are: heating/cooling, transport and power. The proportion of renewable energy is still relatively small in each of them. It seems likely that transport will depend on battery technologies in the short term, with hydrogen increasingly important as the constraints on battery production begin to take effect. The options for renewables sources of energy for heating/cooling and power are more diverse and a range of new technologies is likely to emerge.

One type of renewable energy is biofuels. This also has applications in the transport sector where it is used as an additive to petrol or diesel. It is produced from organic matter, typically recycling waste materials. By substituting for a proportion of the oil-based fuels, it is classified as renewable energy. However, the combustion of the biofuel creates greenhouse gas, although at a lower level than oil-based fuels, and it perpetuates the use of petrol and diesel vehicles. Another reason to be cautious about biofuels is that they are frequently derived from agricultural products that are grown specifically for this market. This leads to land being used for monoculture to meet growing demand for transport energy. This may, in turn, drive up the cost of food if the return on agriculture-for-energy is greater than the return on food production.

The transition to green energy faces major challenges. In February 2021, an article in *Forbes* estimated that fossil fuels accounted for 84 per cent of total energy.[11]

Table 6.2: Percentage consumption of the primary energy sources

Energy source: fossil fuel	%
Oil	33
Coal	27
Natural gas	24
Energy source: non-fossil fuel	
Hydro-electric	6
Other renewables	5
Nuclear	4
Other	1

Source: BP Statistical Review 2020

Energy intensity

One of the challenges facing economies as they move towards net zero will be the need to use energy more efficiently. The concept of energy intensity provides a measure of the energy used to produce a given level of GDP. In essence, economies need to use less energy while they continue to grow. Currently we see total energy demand increasing and this is barely offset by improvements in energy intensity. Energy intensity is improving at a rate of 0.4 per cent, yet if decarbonization targets are to be met this will need to improve to a rate of between 4 and 10 per cent.

Although the measure of energy intensity is used to show that governments are making progress in using energy more efficiently, it can be a misleading indicator. For example, populations might be growing, GDP might be increasing and governments might claim success because the energy intensity measure is moving in the right direction. However, if total CO_2 emissions are still increasing, or only slowly decreasing, then this will not prevent global temperatures from rising. Therefore, any measure of energy intensity needs to be achieved in conjunction with a decline in CO_2 emissions. If we wish to track our progress in preventing global warming, one of the most relevant measures to track is parts per million (ppm) or carbon emissions, expressed relative to the carbon budget.

Parts per million (ppm)

Data on atmospheric CO_2 is frequently measured against a base year, often taken at some point close to the start of the industrial revolution. Atmospheric carbon can be measured over time to assess emission levels.

Table 6.3: Atmospheric parts per million 1870–2019

Year	ppm	Years elapsed	ppm increase	Average per year
1870	290	–	–	–
1920	305	50	15	0.3
1970	320	50	25	0.5
2019	414	50	94	1.9

There is a correlation between ppm and projected increases in global temperatures. In 2019, the rise in global temperatures was approximately 0.8°C. The IPCC provides forecasts on the possible impact of greenhouse gas on future global temperatures. These forecasts are often given as a percentage probability of an outcome, for example a less than 66 per cent chance of exceeding a 2°C rise in global temperatures.

The IPCC Assessment Report, AR5, offers projections for global temperature increases, associated with different ppm.[12]

507 ppm 1.5°C
618 ppm 2.0°C

How soon we reach a particular level of concentration will depend upon the rate at which CO_2 is released into the atmosphere. Current levels are at approximately 3.0 ppm/year, but there is concern that this rate is increasing.

Carbon emissions (carbon budget)

Another measure for tracking the impact of human activity on global warming is to monitor the number of tonnes of CO_2 released into the atmosphere. Again, there is a correlation between the number of tonnes emitted and global temperatures. Data suggests that if the increase in global temperatures is to be limited to 2°C then the total cumulative emissions of CO_2 should not exceed 2,900 billion tonnes. The IPCC estimates that in order to have a 66 per cent chance of meeting a 2°C target, the total cumulative emissions of CO_2 emitted from 1870 onwards needs to remain below 2,900 billion tonnes. Roughly, half this budget was consumed between 1870 and 2000. In the 15 years between 2000 and 2014, more than one third of the remaining carbon budget was consumed. The remaining carbon budget from 2015 onwards (roughly 890 billion tonnes of CO_2) will be consumed in less than 30 years if emissions remain at 2014 levels.

Table 6.4: Forecasting the remaining carbon budget

Period	Billion tonnes CO_2 equivalent
1870–2000	1,545
2001–2014	465
2015–?	890
TOTAL	2,900

Source: Data from IPCC

Information from the IPCC suggests that at the current level of emissions there are approximately 27 years remaining before we exceed the limit of the carbon budget of 2,900 billion tonnes.

The prognosis is not good and the rapid reduction of carbon emissions remains the overriding challenge if we are to reverse climate change. Not only do we need to replace existing carbon emitting electrical generation with renewables, but we also need to provide the additional capacity in electrical generation that will become necessary as we adopt new technologies, such as electric or hydrogen fuelled transport. National governments need to provide the evidence that they have strategies in place to manage this transition and there needs to be global oversight to assess the progress of energy transition at an international level.

7

Moving Away from Growth and Profit

Chapter summary

This chapter examines how economies measure success and how businesses measure profit. The pursuit of profit and the principles of the free market are frequently claimed to be the best mechanisms to allocate resources effectively and ensure a prosperous economy. This chapter considers the flaws in this reasoning: that profit does not measure all relevant costs, most importantly, the environmental cost, nor are market genuinely free as governments frequently intervene with grants, subsidies and tax breaks, with the oil and gas sector being one of the major beneficiaries.

Introduction

The transition to a sustainable society will require a change in our values, attitudes and behaviours. Specifically, we need to move away from values that regard economic growth as a higher priority than the protection of the planet. Our myopic fixation with growth and profit threatens to destroy our civilization. In his book, *Immoderate Greatness: Why Civilisations Fail* (2012) William Ophuls sets out the argument that '... civilisation is effectively hardwired for self-destruction.'

The book provides a compelling analysis of the factors that drive the rise and fall of civilization. Although it offers a pessimistic prognosis for the human race as it enters a spiral of decline, it does at least explain the factors that have driven us to such a sorry state. The book is brilliantly written and it cannot be recommended too highly. Ultimately, the book does offer a glimmer of hope but it suggests that the survival of civilization '... would require a revolution in human thought greater than the one that created the modern world.'[1]

A more optimistic view of the future might argue that we do have the capability to create a civilization that is sustainable – environmentally, economically and societally. Humans have enormous capacity to think creatively, to help others and believe in concepts of fairness. Human society is bound by shared beliefs and values. These drive our attitudes and behaviours. Our challenge is to achieve a shift in society from where it is now to where we would like it to be. The problem is that we cannot expect communities and nations suddenly to reject values that underpin their lives. It takes time to adopt a new set of values; gradual shifts in perceptions will need to be reinforced by an iterative process that encourages new behaviours, and this in turn will reinforce the emerging values.

Any process of social change starts with an awareness of the need to change followed by a change in behaviours and then reinforcement as the new behaviours bring new benefits. For example, ten years ago there was little demand for EV; however, this demand has grown rapidly due to the growing awareness of the environmental damage caused by petrol and diesel vehicles. Social values that might previously have conferred status on people that owned large 4 × 4 gas guzzlers are changing to new social values that are critical of such vehicles. This shift in values creates the opportunity for social and economic change. Action by governments can reinforce this shift in attitudes and behaviours by offering incentives to switch to EV. Over the next few years, we will see more people switch to low emission vehicles and this, in turn, will lead to a corresponding change in values.

The failure of our generation

Since the end of the Second World War, we have seen the natural environment destroyed at an unprecedented rate: rain forests flattened, oceans polluted, the atmosphere damaged. We have seen our social and political systems create great wealth in developed countries, yet millions remain at or below subsistence levels. As individuals, we are caring and compassionate, yet we are often slow to intervene until events affect us personally.

We understand the concept of moral responsibility, yet we hide behind excuses that politicians and vested interests are to blame. While these groups have much to answer for, we cannot absolve ourselves of personal responsibility. We vote for them. We work for them. We buy their products. The moral certitude of the hippy generation seems to have been quickly sacrificed when the opportunity for personal gain presented itself. We need to acknowledge our individual and collective responsibility. More than that, we need to change our patterns of consumption and the things that we aspire to.

The reasons for our collective failure include the following points.

The inability of the individual to affect change

While individuals may accept that modern industrialized economies cause damage to the environment, we feel unable to change things because our individual action to live more sustainably will be inconsequential, yet the impact it has on our lives may be high.

Influence and power

Vested interests, commercial objectives and financial power exert a strong influence on leaders and governments, yet, as individuals, we exert little influence.

Status

Social values and cultural norms are often based on the pursuit of personal wealth and conspicuous consumption. Social status is frequently linked to the cars we drive, the houses we own and the holidays we enjoy.

Attitudes and beliefs

The protestant work ethic pervades many developed Western economies and there is deep-rooted belief in the virtues of hard work, personal advancement and entitlement to material wealth.

Disconnect from the impact of environmental damage

The populations of the industrialized societies are largely disconnected from the natural world and while individuals may be concerned by reports that the Amazon rain forest is being destroyed, there is little impact on us directly.

Visibility and linkage

If there is no obvious connection between our economic activity and its consequences on the environment there will be little reason for governments, organizations or consumers to change their behaviour. Unless we see the linkage between the damage done by industrialized societies there will be little pressure for change.

The pursuit of profit

If we recognize that things have to change then a good place to start is to review the forces that drive our current economic model. Modern industrialized economic activity carries a significant environmental cost, yet this cost is rarely reflected in profit and loss accounts. There are two types of environmental cost that we need to consider: direct and indirect. Direct environmental costs will have a clear and traceable link to commercial activity, while indirect environmental costs are the consequential costs of environmental damage that may have no obvious connection to an organization's commercial activity.

For example, commercial fishing fleets operating off the coast of West Africa are decimating fish stocks. Fish that had previously fed populations across West Africa are now used to produce fishmeal for use as an agricultural feedstock. Fishing communities that once had an abundance of food no longer have enough food to eat. Where they had previously earned income from the sale of fish, they can no longer afford healthcare or education. This is an example of direct environmental costs.

Less obvious are the indirect costs that might result. For example, populations might be forced to move away from coastal communities to search for work in cities or migrate to other countries. Poverty in cities will increase, causing a rise in social unrest and crime. Migration to other countries will change the ethnic and religious balance of communities, potentially triggering political tensions and social unrest. These indirect costs are less obvious than the immediate impact on fishing communities, but these consequential costs could be enormous.

Economic activity will continue to damage the environment until we have a mechanism that holds organizations (and consumers) accountable for the cost of their activity. The argument against this type of *full environmental cost pricing* is that much of what we buy would become unaffordable if companies had to meet the full cost of providing their goods and services. However, the reality is that in many cases it is already unaffordable; it is just that somebody else is paying the price. The countries with emerging economies frequently bear the cost of natural resources being commercially exploited, which means that they are effectively subsidizing low-cost goods for the developed world. At present, we are perpetuating a system that is not only unsustainable but also unjust.

The transition to a sustainable society will require the full environmental cost to be accounted for in the price of goods and services. Living in a sustainable society may mean that we buy fewer *things*. The way that we finance and use products is also likely to change. For example, consumer goods such as domestic equipment and cars may be leased rather than owned. This would encourage manufacturers, who will bear the full lifetime cost of the product, to produce long-lasting, reliable products, with low maintenance costs and the ability to recycle and recover valuable materials at the end of life. These changes will drive restructuring of our economies, see a decline in some types of products and services and create opportunities for new ones.

At an international level, there may be resistance to changes that will adversely affect those nations that built their wealth on exploiting natural resources, mass consumption, short life cycles and disposal at end of life. This desire to protect national economic interests was exemplified in events leading up to the Kyoto Protocol, designed to limit the emission of greenhouse gases, in 1997, when two US Senators, Robert Byrd and Chuck Hagel, put forward a resolution that the US should not be party to any protocol that harmed the US economy. Their resolution was passed unanimously in the senate. In the event, the US Ambassador, Peter Burleigh, did sign the Kyoto Protocol, but resistance to Kyoto continued to impact US environmental policy. This type of resistance is likely to continue while economic growth remains the overriding priority.

Although there is considerable resistance from many parts of the corporate world, other organizations are bold advocates of social and economic change. The last decade has seen many organizations acknowledge the need for social and environmental responsibility. In addition, there is a pragmatic acknowledgement that future legislation and changing patterns of consumer demand will require organizations to operate in ways that are sustainable, prompting many organizations to re-evaluate their environmental impact. This growing organizational focus on environmental and social value is described in the work of John Elkington (2004) and his coining of the term the *triple bottom line.*[2]

The three elements of the triple bottom line are economic value, environmental value and social value. Conventional theories of capitalist behaviour focus on economic value, particularly profit and shareholder returns. Elkington identifies seven drivers of change that will move our economic model towards sustainable capitalism. Elkington's seven drivers of change are:

- Markets: Organization will need to anticipate and respond to changes in regulatory conditions and consumer expectations, specifically the growing concern for the environmental and social impact of the products and services they consume.
- Values: Organizations need to respond to changes in societal values. Those organizations that are perceived as failing to

live out the emerging values of social and environmental responsibility will not only alienate them from their customers at an emotional level, but they risk pursuing inappropriate commercial strategies.

- Transparency: Organizations are facing growing demands for transparency that places them under pressure to demonstrate their social and environmental performance. In the UK, there have been a growing number of new requirements on organization to report on their environmental impact, such as Streamlined Energy and Carbon Report (SECR).[3] This is pushing social and environmental obligations higher up the boardroom agenda and it enables consumers and shareholders to benchmark performance.

- Lifecycle technology: Organizations are under growing pressure to demonstrate ethical practices throughout the whole life cycle of their activities. It is no longer acceptable to source materials or products that have been produced through exploitation of labour or by methods that damage the environment.

- Partners: Organizations will see benefits in working collaboratively. The traditional competitive and potentially exploitative business relationships create costs, friction and conflict. Partnerships allow innovation, shared best practice and opportunities to share costs in developing new technologies. The move towards collaboration will be driven by a shared realization that the environmental threat requires a rapid response and consolidated effort.

- Time: Organizations will need to operate in new ways and on new time scales. The digital economy is increasing the pace of decision-making, enabling more information to be processed in a given period. Elkington describes this as time getting *wider*. In contrast, the nature of decisions being taken by companies will need to focus less on short-term strategies, such as quarterly sales targets, and more on long-term goals, such as the impact of business activity on future generations. Elkington describes this as *long time*.

- Corporate governance: Organizations are already seeing pressure on their executive teams to explain their business purpose; what is the business for? Whose interests does it serve? How is it run? This pressure is affecting the wider supply chains and the business ecosystem. It is affecting the culture of organizations and the characteristics of the people selected to lead them. Managers that might previously have been promoted because they demonstrated appropriate commercial *killer instincts* will need to demonstrate new corporate values.

The concept of the triple bottom line offers a useful model for understanding the drivers of change within organizations. There is no doubt that the business world is going through a commercial and emotional revolution. The new heroes of the corporate world are those leaders driving sustainable and ethical businesses. There are amazing people, doing incredible things that are helping the transformation to a sustainable society. The challenge is to manage the difficult balancing act of pushing new boundaries, creating new markets and investing in new products yet at the same time ensuring that there is a commercial case for the investment required.

Successful transition will require businesses, government, consumers and voters to move in step so that they encourage each other forward but do not get so far out of step that they become isolated. For business, being isolated means investing in products and services that fail to meet consumer requirements. For governments, being isolated means alienation from voters. For consumers, being isolated means that they are *voices in the wilderness*, out of step with society and disillusioned. For voters, being isolated means lacking a political home, potentially resulting in frustration, anger and rebellion.

The rights of future generations

The discussion on sustainability frequently hinges on *who pays*. This is an issue that not only affects the environmental cost of goods and services, but it is also a question of obligations on the current generation to protect future generations, rather than being entitled to exploit natural resources, raise global temperatures and leave a legacy of an unsustainable planet.

The debate also attributes blame to previous generations that exploited natural resources, creating the problems now being faced. If we go back a few thousand years, the Iron Age smelters destroyed forests across Britain and Europe. Similarly, the Romans and their relentless consumption of wood and overworking of the land caused damage to the environment. However, it would be unhelpful for Brazil or Indonesia to justify the destruction of rain forests on the basis that *the Europeans started it*. Clearly, the activities of previous generations do not justify the actions of our current generation.

There is a concern that the developed nations risk being accused of hypocrisy when they demand that emerging economies limit their environmental impact. Why should the developing nations be told to stop cutting down forests or stop burning coal if this is the fastest route to economic growth? Why should nations with emerging economies be denied the opportunity to improve standards of living if this was how nations with advanced economies achieved their wealth? However, the argument that nations with emerging economies are exempt from environmental responsibility until they achieve some form of parity with wealthier nations is framing the problem in the wrong way. Our attention should focus on achieving a *just transition*. How we frame these debates, the questions that we pose and the definitions that we choose to adopt will influence the way that we interpret issues such as *justice* or *blame*. For example, if the question is: *How do we ensure that nations with emerging economies have access to cheap, green energy?* Then the debate might focus on practical actions to ensure the transition to clean energy.

A just transition

The concept of environmental justice relates to how costs or benefits are attributed between nations and communities. The definition of communities might relate to specific communities within an individual nation, geographical location or communities within towns, cities or areas of countryside. The communities might be defined by race, age, income level or other characteristics that might lead to discrimination or exclusion. The risk is that the transition to a sustainable society will create winners and losers, in particular, that the poor and disadvantaged will be the losers.

The hope is that the transition to a sustainable society will create opportunities for economic wealth and improved standards of living and that the process of transition will address existing injustices and inequality. In the UK, there is much discussion about *levelling up.* Although imprecisely defined, this seems to relate to addressing the disparity in wealth between different regions. There is also the aspiration that *green jobs* will create new employment and that reskilling will help the unemployed and those on low wages to find good jobs. All of these things are possible, and the concept of the *Green New Deal* will be explored later in the book.

Responsibility for the cost of environmental damage

Much of our current economic and political thinking is based on the principle that markets operate most effectively when they are allowed to operate freely. The advocates of free-market economics distrust government interference and regulation. The principle that resources are most efficiently allocated when markets are unregulated might be true in the short term, particularly where the measure of success is profitability, but unregulated market forces are not an effective way to achieve sustainable social or environmental outcomes. Neither do they achieve desirable economic outcomes over the longer term. In the fishing example, there will be short-term profits from the exploitation of fish stocks, but the business activity will not be viable once stocks are depleted, and there is no longer an opportunity to make profit.

It is likely that full environmental cost pricing would result in price increases during the short term, but in practice, organizations would be encouraged to find alternative ways to meet consumer demand, and companies would seek out alternative, more sustainable ways of meeting the demands of the market. For example, a producer of fishmeal might find ways to process waste food that had previously been uneconomic to use.

Purpose beyond profit

As previously discussed, addressing the causes of climate change and environmental damage will require a move towards full environmental cost accounting, also referred to as *externalities*. This will drive commercial organizations to develop sustainable business models rather than short-term, profit maximizing models. This type of *green accounting* will create a visible link between economic activity and environmental costs, but ultimately, organizations need to go beyond compliance with accounting standards and regulations. The next stage is for organizations to fulfil a social purpose. This sentiment is captured in the phrase: *Doing less bad is not good enough.*

Genuinely sustainable organizations will seek to achieve beneficial outcomes for both the environment and for the wider society. Profit will not be an end in itself, but rather it will be the enabler that allows organizations to continue to serve their social purpose. The concept of organizations fulfilling social purpose is not new or radical. Many organizations will consider social obligations as part of their strategic objectives. However, there needs to be a shift in organizational strategy that regards profit as the priority and social obligations as secondary. There needs to be a shift to a strategic mindset that places social and environmental obligations as the driving purpose with profit being the commercial mechanism that enables these activities to continue.

Growth is not the goal

Our current economic system is based on the fallacy of continual growth and it uses measures of success that fail to take account of the negative consequences of our actions. We need to reappraise growth and profit as objectives and adopt more appropriate measures that will help us move towards a more equitable and sustainable economic system. We cannot continue to extol an economic system that is driving the planet to the edge of destruction. We have to change our assumptions about society and the economic system that sustains it. This will require building new social and economic models that are compatible with sustainable development.

Continued focus on industrial growth is economically unsustainable as resources will become increasingly scarce and costs will increase to the point where many products regarded as affordable today will become luxuries in the future. Increased GDP does not necessarily result in a growth in living standards across society. Nations can achieve a growth in economic wealth, but the benefits of this wealth might go to an increasingly small proportion of the population. The experience of the last couple of decades is that many countries have seen a growing wealth gap between the top 5 per cent and the majority that have experienced a decline in their standard of living.

A report by the UN Department of Social and Economic Affairs, the World Social Report 2020: *Inequality in a Rapidly Changing World* provides a concise and very readable summary of the issues. The overall assessment is given in the executive summary, partially quoted below:

> Income inequality has increased in most developed countries and in some middle-income countries, including China and India, since 1990. Countries where inequality has grown are home to more than two thirds (71 per cent) of the world population. Yet growing inequality is not a universal trend. The Gini coefficient of income inequality has declined in most countries of Latin America and the Caribbean and in several African and Asian countries over the last two decades.
>
> Despite progress in some countries, income and wealth are increasingly concentrated at the top. The share of income going to the richest 1 per cent of the population increased in 59 out of 100 countries with data from 1990 to 2015. Meanwhile, the poorest 40 per cent earned less than 25 per cent of income in all 92 countries with data.[4]

It is important to distinguish *quantitative* measures, such as the rate of increase in GDP, and *qualitative* measures, which describe the quality of life. The real problem of using GDP to measure growth is that it does not tell us much about the quality of life.

Adopting relevant measures

As mentioned above, there is a need for visibility and linkage. It is only when we have visibility of the impact of our actions and when we understand the linkage between actions and outcomes that we will be able to take appropriate corrective action. Governments and organizations need to adopt reporting mechanisms that enable this visibility. Relevant measures will provide information on issues such as:

- Rate of consumption of natural resources.
- The emission of greenhouse gases.
- Environmental damage.
- Quality of life for individuals and communities.

The characteristics of effective measures will include their ability to:

- Demonstrate a linkage between outcome and cause.
- Enable informed political and corporate decisions to reduce adverse environmental impact.
- Reveal the interdependencies between economic activity and environmental damage.

In 2011, the European Union proposed a set of indicators relevant to the social and environmental challenges facing society. The following is quoted from an article dated 27 April 2011 in Greenbiz.com: 'In its 2009 Communication "GDP and Beyond: Measuring progress in a changing world," the European Commission proposed five actions as part of the EU roadmap for the development of indicators relevant to the challenges of today.' The five indicators are:

1. Complementing GDP with environmental and social indicators.
2. Near real-time information for decision-making.
3. More accurate reporting on distribution and inequalities.
4. Developing a European Sustainable Development Scoreboard.
5. Extending national accounts to environmental and social issues.

The article went on to say:

> A key element of the communication is that the time is ripe for measurement systems to shift emphasis from measuring economic production to measuring people's well-being. This theme was also explored in a report presented to the Franco-German Ministerial Council in December 2010. This proposed a compact dashboard of indicators that assess human welfare. And three major areas – economic performance, quality of life and sustainability – were identified in a report by the Commission on the Measurement of Economic Performance and Social Progress – a French government initiative launched in 2008.
>
> [...]Using a framework of green accounting would mean that investment decisions are made by comparing the overall private and social costs against the private and social benefits. Using a lifecycle assessment means that organizations can make decisions based on calculating environmental impacts at every stage of a product's life, from raw materials, through production, distribution and final disposal or recycling. With the EU set to introduce more environmental accounting at national level – see 'GDP and Beyond' below – this could filter down to the corporate enterprise level. Increased consumer, citizen and shareholder awareness of sustainable green growth requires a pricing policy that fully reflects the true costs of development. Transparent green accounts would be a key component of a policy based on Beyond GDP.[5]

A sustainable economic model will require financial reporting that measures the impact of commercial activity on the environment. These ideas should not be seen as the revolutionary overthrow of capitalism but a desire for a commercially based economy that is environmentally sustainable.

A socially responsible market economy

The first step is to ensure that any measure of profit takes account of environmental cost. The next step might be to evolve an economic model where organizations are rewarded not in terms of *profit* but in terms of their *social value*. Is it possible to have a not-for-profit market economy? Could commercial organizations move to a not-for-profit business model? Clearly, commercial organizations need to make a financial return but if the uncontrolled pursuit of profit leads to the destruction of the planet then something needs to change.

The process of change needs to be an evolution of current business practices and values, rather than a revolution. The first step in this process of evolution will be accountability for environmental and social cost. The real cost, including environmental and social cost would be reflected within profit and loss reporting. In addition, organizations should report to shareholders (and consumers) using a range of key indicators to produce a *balanced scorecard* that tracks corporate performance on issues relating to social and environmental factors. This type of reporting has strong parallels with the Norton-Kaplan balanced scorecard. The Norton-Kaplan Balanced Scorecard is a strategic management and planning method that tracks short-term and long-term objectives against four distinct organizational perspectives: financial, customer, internal, learning. Each perspective is aligned to organizational vision and strategy.

Visibility of corporate performance would offer benefits to a range of different stakeholders:

- Consumers: Make well-informed purchase decisions.
- Employees: Give assurance of purpose and environmental responsibility.
- Shareholders: Assess compatibility with investment criteria.
- Financial institutions: Assess exposure to risks.
- Governments: Inform policy decisions.

Financial transition

The structure of our financial markets drives an economic system that results in economic cycles of short-term growth followed by recession. It also encourages organizations to seek quick returns at the expense of long-term objectives. As we saw in the 2008 financial crisis, governments protected the financial sector from the worst consequences of the crash. While it was necessary to bail out the banks to prevent an implosion of our financial systems, the financial support was offered virtually unconditionally. We missed an opportunity to reform the financial system by making the financial bailout dependent upon changes within the financial markets. Instead, the system has continued to adopt the same business model and we have learnt few lessons from the crisis. At the time of writing, we once again see that consumer credit is growing rapidly and there are worrying signs that another financial crisis is looming on the horizon.

The move towards a sustainable global society will require a radical review of the way that the financial markets operate and there are a number of areas where changes might be achieved.

- Dampen volatility: Instigate tax structures that reward long-term investment. Correspondingly, discourage short-term and micro-financial trades by applying short-term trading taxes so that trader margins are erased and medium to longer-term investment encouraged.
- Reduce tax avoidance: Tighter regulations to ensure that major organizations pay a fair rate of tax and have less scope to avoid tax obligations through intricate company structures and offshore accounts.
- Transparent banking: Introduce stricter regulations that prevent money laundering and tax avoidance through the use of tax havens.
- Capital markets: Dampen volatility by requiring a sizeable proportion of a company's shares have to be held for a minimum period of time.

- Corporate reporting: Require annual reports to assess if short-term profit projections are at the expense of long-term strategic objectives.

- Consumer credit: Greater accountability on financial organizations to ensure that borrowers do not take on unaffordable levels of debt.

- Financial reporting: Companies obliged to include statements relating to sustainability and environmental impact of business activities.

As already stressed throughout this book, we need to find ways to leverage the strengths of our economic system in order to drive the changes that are required. The goal is not to overthrow capitalism but rather to reform the capitalist model so that growth and profit are not seen as an end in itself but as the means to achieve the goal.

This concept of using the inherent characteristics of the market economy to drive change in our economic system is set out in a book by Sir Ronald Cohen: *Impact: Reshaping Capitalism To Drive Real Change.*[6] Sir Ronald's expertise as a venture capitalist and private equity investor has shaped his ideas and provides a detailed understanding of how financial markets operate. One of the key themes in his book is that business growth requires investment; if we change the criteria that investors use for their investment decisions, we can channel investment into business activity that is environmentally accountable and away from business activities that is damaging. He quotes a depressing statistic that over 250 of the major global corporates cause environmental damage that is greater than the value of their profits. He argues that if these environmental costs are included in corporate accounting then investors will be able to make informed decisions. This concept of *impact weighted accounts* will encourage investment in sustainable business and drive a race to the top rather than a race towards environmental destruction.

This idea of government introducing new regulations to drive changes in investor behaviour is not new. In 1929, following the financial crash, investors realized that the information in company accounts was poorly regulated and was produced to inconsistent standards. This meant that organizations were able to disguise the reality of their financial health and investors had little reliable information on which to base their investment decisions. In 1933, the US government imposed regulations to ensure consistent accounting standards and provided investors with a reasonable level of financial transparency.

The transition to a sustainable, net zero, economy will require massive injections of low-cost finance for emergent technologies and innovative organizations. It will require finance to support major technological change and capital markets will need to divert resources away from traditional industries, moving instead into emergent industries. The cost of borrowing will need to need to be kept low and this may require national governments to underwrite investment in order to reduce the risk carried by the financial sector.

The role of intergovernmental organizations in funding the transition will be critical. Historically, the World Bank has tended to fund programmes that are consistent with Western government foreign policy and encouraged recipient countries to pursue programmes that deliver economic growth. While such programmes achieved economic prosperity for some sectors of these economies, they could also cause problems, particularly in terms of their environmental impact. For example, hydroelectric dams displacing communities and flooding valleys and agricultural programmes that impacted on rain forests in South America and Asia. At the time, such programmes were seen as key to raising economic prosperity. Going forward, The World Bank may need to reassess its purpose, how it operates and the capabilities that it requires. The criteria for funding emergent economies may need to shift away from economic growth and focus on programmes that are consistent with sustainable development in order to address the threat of climate change and protect the natural environment.

Social transition

There is a fundamental incompatibility between a sustainable society and a society that aspires to conspicuous wealth. Moving away from an economy dependent on continual growth will require changes in our patterns of consumption and, more importantly, changes in consumer expectations. Shifting social expectations will be difficult, particularly in those societies where consumerism is closely linked with self-fulfilment. Achieving a social change will require an understanding of the linkage between the current economic system and environmental destruction. Although there is a growing awareness that climate change is a potential problem, for most people in the advanced economies it is a theoretical issue and the linkage between lifestyle and environmental impact is not immediately obvious.

Unless there is greater voter awareness of the linkage between climate change and the issues impacting their daily lives then there will be little political pressure to address the underlying causes. Instead, the political debate will focus on actions that supress the symptoms but do nothing to prevent the problems getting worse.

8

Factors Critical to Successful Change

Chapter summary

This chapter considers the factors that enable change to happen and examines where the pressure for the transition to a sustainable society is likely to come from. It looks at the capabilities that will be required to manage radical change successfully and offers a method of categorizing three essential capabilities. The chapter concludes with the proposition that ultimately, the process of social transition requires a shift in attitudes and beliefs at an emotional level not simply an acceptance of scientific evidence and data.

An unprecedented challenge

The size of the task that lies ahead, coupled with the limited time to achieve the changes will require exceptional political, corporate and civic leadership. The scale of change will be unprecedented in peacetime, although historically we know that countries can achieve rapid social and economic change during times of war. Anyone with experience of corporate change will know the difficulties of adopting new technologies, implementing new corporate structures and embedding a new organizational culture. Added to this are all the issues associated with programme governance, budgets and corporate politicking. Corporate change is difficult, but managing global economic, political and social transformation is on an entirely different scale.

In the build-up to the year 2000 (Y2K) there were concerns that the millennium bug would affect computer systems, leading to lurid predictions that business systems would crash, cars would suddenly stop and aircraft would fall from the sky. To avert these potential doomsday scenarios, many organizations replaced their IT systems and used the opportunity to restructure and streamline their operations.

The big consultancies had a bonanza and frantically recruited consultants to meet the massive jump in demand for their services. The result was that there was a boom period for consulting from about 1995 to 2005 and new roles emerged within organizations as they recognized the need for greater internal capability to manage rapid technical and organizational change. Organizational systems became highly integrated, cloud computing took off and business processes became harmonized between organizations. Within ten years, we saw a step-change in organizational efficiency, new roles, new skills and the creation of a truly integrated, global economy.

The emergence of Y2K was a potential threat to our modern economy, and the technological changes of that time offer an analogy for the challenges associated with climate change. Responding to the challenge of Y2K required significant cost and disruption, but the emerging threat presented an opportunity to do things better. One of the major obstacles for organizations was the lack of expertise to manage and implement the changes required within the limited time available. In the short term, organizations were able to fill this gap by employing external consultants, but over time, they recruited new people and developed expertise within their organizations. They not only developed the technical skills, but they also developed the methodology and processes to manage corporate change.

In seeking to understand the factors critical to successful change, it is important to distinguish two types of expertise:

1. Task expertise.
2. Process expertise.

Task expertise

This refers to the skills, knowledge and experience necessary to achieve the required change. It will include technical expertise such as the ability to develop and deploy the technologies associated with renewable energy, digital power grids, waste management, electrical vehicles and so forth. Task expertise provides answers to questions related to *what* needs to be done.

Process expertise

This relates to the expertise necessary to manage the process of change, particularly when groups are in *complexity* and *uncertainty*. Process expertise provides answers to questions that relate to *how* things need to be done. It will include expertise such as the ability to identify strategic options, build consensus, engage with stakeholders and facilitate change.

To appreciate the relevance of *process expertise* and to understand how it differs from *task expertise*, it is worth diverting into a brief review of certainty, complexity and uncertainty.[1]

Certainty, complexity and uncertainty

Each of these three states can be described as follows:

- Certainty: We know the question. We know the answer.
- Complexity: We need to clarify the question. We can find the answer.
- Uncertainty: We don't know the question. The answer is unknown.

Task expertise is very effective in situations of *certainty*. For example, a local authority might need to estimate the annual cost of maintenance on its fleet of EV; it knows how many vehicles it owns and the approximate annual cost of maintenance per vehicle.

In a situation of *complexity*, a local authority might face the question: *How many electric vehicle charging points do we need to install in the city centre during the next five years?* This is a clearly defined question and to find the answer the local authority can employ experts with knowledge of electric vehicle charging infrastructure and demand forecasting. Task expertise is effective in situations where the question is defined and the relevant information can be identified.

However, task expertise is not very effective in situations of *uncertainty*. For example, a large city might wish to publish a future transport strategy. To develop such a strategy it will be necessary to identify the questions that need to be addressed. However, actually defining the questions may be difficult. One question might be: *How many privately owned EV will be on the roads in 10 years?* But is this the right question? Maybe EV will be superseded by hydrogen technologies. Maybe private ownership will be rare in cities. Maybe the questions might include:

- What proportion of city residents will own vehicles?
- Should cities restrict the use of private vehicles and invest in improved public transport?
- Will autonomous vehicles replace private ownership?
- Will the shift to home working affect demand for public transport?

It quickly becomes apparent that we are in *uncertainty* when we do not know which questions need to be answered, and we certainly do not know the answers. Working in *uncertainty* is likely to start with divergent thinking (to explore the boundaries of possibility), and this will then be followed by convergent thinking (to assess, weight, prioritize and rank these different possibilities). In these situations, *process expertise* is required. This relates to the capability to manage processes that enable individuals and groups to be creative, to assimilate ideas, to assess options, define strategies and agree action plans. In broad terms, the process of guiding groups through uncertainty is often described as *facilitation.*

Process expertise works in conjunction with task expertise; it is not a replacement for it. The role of the task expert will be to build on the available knowledge to address specific questions at various stages in the process. For example, the task expert would need to provide advice on the pros and cons of emerging technologies so that the process of prioritizing and ranking different possibilities can be based on the best available information. The role of the process expert is to manage *how* teams are working in situations where the task experts cannot simply provide *the answer*. Indeed, in situations of complexity and uncertainty there is a significant risk in expecting a task expert to provide *the answer*, not least because the question being presented to the task expert may be the wrong question.

One of the conundrums is that groups and organizations frequently fail to recognize when they are in uncertainty. All too often, there is an assumption that *we understand the question and we know – or can find – the answer*. Consequently, the relevant experts are instructed to *solve the problem* until, at some point, it becomes apparent that things are more complicated than originally anticipated.

Groups that rely on *task expertise* to address *complex* or *uncertain* problems will eventually run into difficulties and become dysfunctional. Typical symptoms will be:

• The task leader and other participants become frustrated.
• Disagreements break out.
• Blame is attributed.
• Emotions run high.
• Little progress is made.
• The quality of outcomes is poor.

At some point, the group will decide that things are not working. If they are able to recognize that the problem is due to the level of uncertainty then they may be able to recover the situation by employing *process expertise*, rather than relying on *task expertise*. Unfortunately, groups often fail to recognize that they are operating in uncertainty and their frustration results in other people being blamed; *they don't know what they are talking about*. Consequently, the response to the problem might be to get rid of one group of experts, bring in another group of experts and hope that the newly appointed incumbent can provide the answer.

Process aware

The first requirement of any government or organization leading a process of change is the ability to understand the difference between certainty, complexity and uncertainty. The second requirement is that leaders and organizations have the ability to operate in uncertainty by using *process* expertise, not simply relying on *task* expertise. The ability to distinguish certainty, complexity and uncertainty, coupled with the ability to adopt appropriate strategies in situations of uncertainty is defined as *process aware*.

Having worked as a facilitator advising on strategic change in both the public and private sectors for many years, it is my experience that most managers have little formal training in these techniques. Fortunately, many people are quickly aware when problems occur and will have the emotional intelligence and personality to work collaboratively to find ways around problems. However, while good interpersonal skills might help address some problems within dysfunctional groups, there will be situations where the root cause of the problem needs to be addressed. Where groups continue to battle on, determined to make progress, they risk making poor decisions.

The characteristics of successful change

While studying for an MBA, I undertook research to identify the characteristics of successful change. This involved detailed reviews of eight public sector change projects, comparing projects that were regarded as successful with those that failed to deliver some or all of the required outcomes. The findings identified three primary factors associated with successful projects:

- Effective leadership.
- Effective engagement.
- Effective delivery.

In those projects that were successful, all three factors were demonstrated. In projects that were not successful, one or more of these factors failed to be demonstrated effectively. It is important to note that *process expertise* is required in each of these three factors. The following section examines each of these three factors in more detail.

1. Effective leadership

The results from the research identified specific characteristics relating to leadership. Successful projects shared common leadership characteristics, and unsuccessful projects failed to exhibit the same characteristics. These characteristics can be regarded as *hygiene* factors in the sense that they have to be present in order to achieve successful outcomes.

The characteristics of effective leadership include:

- Actions consistent with words: Behaviours that build trust and legitimacy.
- Vision for the organization: Able to define and communicate the vision.
- Open and honest: Recognized as open, honest and acting with integrity.
- Authority: Leaders provide clear authority for the required changes.
- Support: Leaders act when issues are escalated, and they provide support to those implementing the change.

Projects where these characteristics are absent will encounter problems due to lack of trust, lack of direction and the behaviours associated with a blame culture.

There is an interdependency between these factors. For example, if there is doubt about the future vision, or if the actions of the leaders are inconsistent with the messages, then stakeholders interpret this as a sign that leaders are not committed to the change. If leaders are perceived as uncommitted, then stakeholders will be reluctant to take risks or make decisions. Similarly, it is imperative that managers and teams feel supported by senior leadership. Otherwise, they will be reluctant to take accountability since failure will result in blame.

When leaders are operating in *certainty*, they will draw on their acquired experience and task expertise. However, during times of *uncertainty*, previous experience and task expertise is no longer sufficient and process expertise becomes essential. Effective leaders therefore need the ability to design and manage how teams work; in its broadest sense, this can be defined as facilitation skills. Effective facilitation enables groups to:

- Define the objectives.
- Enable participants to contribute knowledge and expertise.
- Evaluate options, prioritize choices and define actions.
- Manage differences of opinion and avoid destructive conflict.

All these activities need to be free from bias, vested interests and groupthink. If they are not, then clearly the quality of the decisions being taken will be at risk. The following examples highlight the types of behaviour that are likely to lead to poor quality decisions:

- Leaders proclaim to know the answers.
- Leaders make decisions without reference to relevant data.
- Leaders ignore the views of experts or colleagues.
- Leaders allow data to be manipulated and distorted to fit their preferred options.
- Leaders are vulnerable to the opinions of vested interests.

2. Effective engagement

The ability to identify and involve relevant stakeholders is the second of the key factors associated with successful change and it is important to recognize that this condition can only be fulfilled if the first condition of effective leadership is met.

The objective of the engagement process is partly about building support and consensus for the change, but equally important is the need to gather knowledge and expertise from a broad spectrum of stakeholders. As a result, the process of engagement will identify genuine concerns or obstacles that could prevent successful achievement of the objectives.
The characteristics of effective engagement are:

- Relevant stakeholders are identified and involved.
- Leaders and managers actively seek input.
- Stakeholders are able to voice concerns.

- Concerns are listened to and evaluated.
- The engagement process seeks agreement on options.

Effective engagement enables stakeholders to:

- Understand the reasons why change is important.
- Understand the potential implications of change.
- Contribute knowledge and experience to guide the process of change.
- Become advocates for the proposed change.

Engagement activities require all relevant stakeholders to be identified. Once identified, stakeholders will commonly be represented on some form of stakeholder map. This will enable an assessment of issues such as:

- How are they are impacted by the change?
- How can their knowledge and experience best be utilized to achieve a successful outcome?
- What level of resistance/support might they offer?

Clearly, the capability to manage an effective engagement process is key. This means that those responsible for the engagement process will require facilitative techniques in situations of complexity and uncertainty. In addition, it is important to recognize that even the most brilliant engagement processes will fail unless the conditions for effective leadership are in place. Without effective leadership, stakeholders will be sceptical about the purpose of the engagement process. Effective leadership gives legitimacy to the engagement process and builds trust in the purpose, which in turn builds commitment to the outcomes.

3. Effective delivery

The final characteristic of successful change is the ability to manage the delivery of the change. The characteristics of effective delivery include:

- Governance and programme management capabilities to ensure appropriate direction and control.
- Technical capabilities relevant to the changes to be implemented.
- Management capabilities to ensure that changes are implemented.

Effective delivery will require managing changes associated with:

- New strategic goals.
- New organizational structures.
- New systems and processes.
- New roles.
- New behaviours and organizational culture.

Leadership, engagement and delivery

It is important to recognize that all three factors, *leadership*, *engagement* and *delivery* capabilities have to be in place. For example, the *leadership* team could be highly competent and inspirational; the *delivery* team could have all the technical skills required to implement the changes, but the project would fail without effective *engagement* to ensure that everyone involved supported the changes, contributed their knowledge and acted as advocates.

Managing a process of change, whether that is managing Brexit, driving improvements in the NHS or transitioning to a zero-carbon economy, will require the capabilities to fulfil all three factors. Organizations are generally very good at operating in certainty, but they frequently perform poorly in complexity and uncertainty. As the operating environment becomes increasingly uncertain, there are likely to be greater strains on each of these three factors. The relationship between these three critical success factors is illustrated in Figure 8.1.

In each of the three factors, leadership, engagement, delivery, process expertise is essential. For example, effective *leadership* requires the ability to develop the vision, communicate it and behave in ways that are 'open and honest'. Leaders with good process skills will be seen as confident operating in new and uncharted territories; they might not have the answers, but they work effectively in developing options and building on the knowledge of those around them. This builds legitimacy and trust.

Figure 8.1: Factors enabling successful change

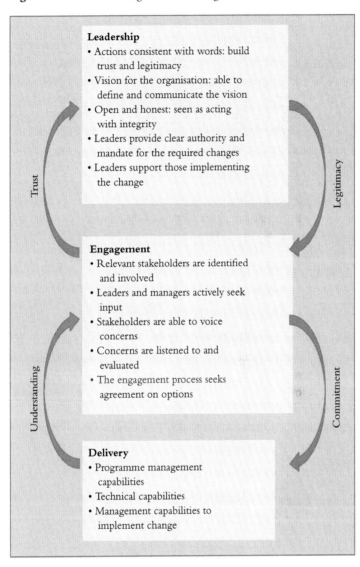

Source: Richard Joy

Where leaders lack effective process skills, it is unlikely that they will perform well in conditions of complexity or uncertainty. Leaders who rely on *task* expertise will only feel comfortable in situations where the question is clear and they know the answer; typically, they like to be in control and they will tell people what to do. Leaders without process skills will appear *out of their depth* when they are required to operate in complexity and uncertainty. Consequently, they are likely to adopt behaviours that are less than open, honest or transparent and they will lack legitimacy.

Similarly, effective engagement requires *process* skills (facilitation skills) to identify stakeholders, seek input and identify options. It is particularly important that dissenting voices are heard and the reasons understood. Any process of change is, by its nature, operating in complexity and uncertainty. Therefore, any attempt to implement a predetermined solution is likely to fail as this assumes that the questions are defined and the answers are known. In reality, this is unlikely, therefore it has to be assumed that a range of options needs to identified and evaluated. It may well be that the eventual option is different to earlier expectations. An effective process of engagement will result in commitment, not only by those that will be impacted by the changes but also by those that are implementing the changes.

The third factor, delivery, will also require effective process expertise. Those teams implementing the changes will also be operating in uncertainty, facing new challenges and required to make decisions when the questions and answers are not clear, therefore, effective process skills will again be required.

Global change capabilities

The challenge of transitioning to a sustainable society is enormous and will require the intergovernmental organizations, national governments and major corporations to build their capabilities across each of these three critical factors. Some organizations will have strengths in some of these areas, for example, the World Bank may be excellent at managing programmes, and national governments will be able to draw on a wealth of delivery expertise to address the technical aspects of moving towards a low carbon society. However, achieving a successful transition to a sustainable society will require not just *delivery* capabilities, such as technical expertise in renewable energy, green transport and smart cities, but it will also require *leadership* and *engagement* capabilities. All three of these capabilities need to be underpinned by *process* expertise.

Epiphany

The process of change is usually triggered by opportunities and threats. If there is no perceived reason to change, most individuals or organizations will allow the status quo to perpetuate. If governments, corporations or communities are to respond to the challenge of climate change, they need a compelling reason to change. Such reasons for change might be evidence based or they might be driven by an emotional conviction. The most powerful reasons for change will draw on both evidence and emotion. Even where there is compelling evidence, the change will only be sustained if it is supported by an emotional commitment.

It is difficult to use evidence alone to persuade people to change their attitudes and behaviours because one of the characteristics of the human mind is that it attempts to make the evidence fit personal perceptions and beliefs rather than the other way around. If this were not the case, we would have to continually readjust our personal paradigm in the light of new information. Therefore, when people are presented with new evidence, they are likely to perform mental gymnastics to make the evidence fit existing beliefs rather than acknowledge a flaw in their current beliefs. In fact, the process of repeatedly bombarding someone with evidence which conflicts with their existing beliefs is that it can actually reinforce their beliefs as they repeatedly persuade themselves that they are right – and the evidence is wrong.

People that hold the view that *climate change is a hoax* are unlikely to change their minds simply because someone tells them that scientists have evidence of global warming. Instead, they are likely to regard any attempt to change their views with resistance, potentially even regarding it as another example of people perpetuating the hoax.

Achieving a shift in perceptions requires some form of personal experience or encounter with a situation that triggers an emotional connection. This trigger might be the result of a visit to another country and seeing how other people's lives are directly affected by climate change; it might be the result of seeing a documentary that raises concerns; it might be a discussion with a trusted friend or colleague. A radical shift in a person's perceptions, beliefs and values can be described as an *epiphany*. Evidence and data might be a part of that epiphany, but the real emotional change will come when people have a personal experience that challenges their previous paradigms.

Many of us will go to great lengths to isolate ourselves from the unpleasant aspects of society, such as crime, poverty or the effects of war in some distant land. Similarly, we prefer not to reflect too deeply on the potential consequences of ever-increasing global temperatures and damage to the environment. However, the more we isolate ourselves from the reality of climate change the longer it will be before we accept the need for change. We can be told about the consequences of global warming and we might see pictures of polar bears struggling to survive as the ice breaks up. These things are upsetting but we are slow to take action until things affect us personally.

Although there is overwhelming scientific evidence that climate change threatens the future of the planet, many in society prefer to continue with things the way they are rather than face disruption and uncertainty, and there is still little pressure on politicians to implement radical social and economic change. This may be because the consequences of climate change do not affect people directly. Maybe there is a belief that somebody is dealing with the problem and everything will be all right. Maybe there is also a sense that people feel powerless and prefer to look away rather than struggle hopelessly against an overwhelming force.

At some point however, climate change will affect large proportions of the global population and there will be a collective realization that our civilization is at risk. Unfortunately, human nature does not always respond rationally to difficult situations. We seek simple solutions rather than seek to understand the complexities of the challenges that face us, and we seek out targets to blame, such as immigrants, foreigners or the political establishment. As fears grow, society risks breaking into opposing factions that will fan the flames of protest and social unrest. This spiralling societal collapse is described in the final chapter of *Immoderate Greatness*.

> Moreover, although collapse may be foreordained, its course and timing are largely unpredictable. Collapse could happen suddenly or gradually, sooner or later, so why act now? To make matters worse, preparing for this uncertain future requires present sacrifice – that is, the diversion of resources from both current consumption and from the task of coping with today's problems – at a time when those very same resources are becoming scarcer and more expensive. In short, denial, invasion, and procrastination are all but inevitable.

9

Barriers to Change

Chapter summary

This chapter examines the reasons behind the depressing level of political inertia and our failure to respond to the climate emergency with the level of urgency that is required. Politicians seem unable to reject the mantra that economic growth is good, and consumers appear unwilling to adopt more sustainable lifestyles.

The longer we delay, the greater the scale of social change that will be required to transition to a net zero society and the more difficult it will be to manage a globally coordinated response. The problem is that civilization is caught in a trap; climate change will increasingly disrupt our economies. Societies will become more fragmented and political instability will increase, making it ever more difficult to coordinate an effective global political response.

Introduction

Over many years, we have seen a procession of high-level forums where global leaders meet to discuss matters of international importance. At such events climate change is high on the agenda, yet in spite of all the conferences, commitments and good intentions, the level of greenhouse gas emissions continues to rise as global leaders prevaricate. This woeful inertia has gone on for too long. The next few years will require a dramatic shift in political thinking accompanied by an international commitment to action. However, if political leaders are to agree on a clear plan of action there are number of significant barriers that will need to be addressed. This chapter considers some of these barriers and considers whether it is likely that they will be overcome.

Barrier 1: The political dilemma

Since the end of the Second World War, the advanced economies have enjoyed a plentiful supply of affordable consumer goods, made possible by cheap fossil fuels and the relentless exploitation of natural resources. However, this is unsustainable and the transition to a sustainable society will require a fundamental restructuring of an economic model that is based on consumerism. At present, it is virtually unthinkable that any politician would commit to such action as this would risk confrontation with the corporate world and alienate their electorate. However, we are rapidly approaching the point where our current economic model *has* to change. The question is at what point will political parties see electoral advantage in advocating the sustainability agenda?

There is a risk that the political landscape will divide between those parties advocating continued industrial economic growth, and those parties advocating the transition to a sustainable economic model. Ultimately, this means that the ability of humanity to respond to the climate crisis may depend on which political message is promoted more effectively in those countries that have the greatest potential to reverse climate change – and the US is probably the single most important nation in this respect.

The American election at the end of 2020 was a defining moment in the battle to reverse climate change and it was an election characterized by deep division. Studies conducted by Pew Research Centre, based in Washington, US, investigated the division in American politics. The research found that approximately 90 per cent of both Trump and Biden supporters believed that if the opposing candidate wins, it would result in lasting harm to the country.[1]

The three areas where there was greatest concern that the other party would cause harm to the country were the COVID-19 outbreak, healthcare and the economy. The extent to which the environment was seen to be tied to the economy was not clear from the research but we do know that Biden and Trump have very different views on the environment. Perhaps the greatest achievement of the Biden administration will be to position the climate crisis within the American psyche as the single biggest threat to American society. If this happens then it would require both Republicans and Democrats to campaign in 2024 on a ticket of protecting the environment. Sustainable growth could become the battleground where each party strives to demonstrate that they can deliver green economic prosperity. This *fighting over the same turf* would reflect the situation in the UK where all parties strive to demonstrate their commitment to the NHS.

However, the economic downturn experienced by parts of America will be nothing compared to the impact on society when climate change begins to wreak havoc. Unless action is taken to prevent continued global warming, the political establishment will, quite understandably, be blamed, and alternative, potentially extreme, political movements will gain support. Anarchy will replace social order and demagogues promising simplistic solutions will rise to power. As social and political disruption increases there will be greater tension between communities; nations will become isolationist and any hope of an internationally coordinated transition will evaporate.

We are facing two dilemmas: political and economic.

- The political dilemma: politicians will not challenge our existing economic model, as this would be political suicide, but if politicians fail to take action now, they will be displaced by alternative, potentially extremist leaders.
- The economic dilemma: the corporate world is clinging to an economic model that is destined to fail, but the longer the delay, the greater the scale of economic collapse.

Barrier 2: Economic dependency on oil

The oil industry is the foundation stone of the modern economy. Major industries are dependent on it, financial markets have relied on it and international political allegiances are bound by it.

The financial viability of an oil corporation is dependent upon the valuation of the hydrocarbon reserves that it owns and the potential valuation of exploration rights. If the price of oil goes down, the valuation of these assets goes down and sooner or later liabilities will exceed assets. It is not just the financial health of the oil companies that is affected by fluctuations in the market price of oil. The industry is intricately connected to every aspect of the global economy. Small disruptions to price can have significant consequences. Large fluctuations threaten the economic stability of nations. In 2008, following the financial crash, the price of oil fell from $130 per barrel, down to $40 per barrel. During this period, some oil producing states were haemorrhaging their national reserves at a rate that risked bankrupting their economies. It is not surprising that politicians and leaders of the corporate world are keen to see the oil industry protected.

Barrier 3: Political ideology

The scale of the economic transition over the next decade will require significant government intervention. However, capitalist or right-wing ideologies frequently reject high levels of state intervention on the principle that government intervention disrupts market forces, which in turn damages economic wealth. The socialist or left-wing ideologies are more likely to advocate greater levels of state intervention on the principle that market forces alone are not sufficient to provide the desired social and economic outcomes. National politics is invariably coloured by how these ideologies are used to justify policy decisions, and while it is useful for political parties to present themselves as supporters of a capitalist economy or advocates for a socialist society, it is important that ideological dogma does not become a mantra to justify all decisions.

I encountered what appeared to be an example of political ideology determining policy when I attended an event at the Houses of Parliament in 2018 where the panel of speakers included a government minister and a representative from a major energy supplier. The energy minister and the energy company representative both emphasized the need to supply cheap energy to the consumer. During questions, I suggested that providing the cheapest energy was not the only consideration and that the priority was to achieve a rapid switch to renewables, requiring government intervention. My comments were listened to politely but rebuffed on the basis that market forces would produce a better outcome.

Clearly, there will be situations where market forces do achieve desirable outcomes and many of the proposals in this book are based on the ability of market forces to drive change, but there are also times where market intervention can be used to accelerate change faster than would happen by relying on market forces alone. Although the minister emphasized the value of market forces over intervention, there are other situations where free-market ideologies are perfectly happy to intervene to support specific market sectors, for example, the oil industry. An extract from an article by Clive Lewis in *The Guardian*, provides just one example of how government policy supports the oil sector:

Why are taxpayers subsidising the oil and gas companies that jeopardise our future?

A few weeks ago, lost in the never-ending fog of Brexit, the cross-party public accounts committee released a damning report on the public cost of decommissioning oil and gas infrastructure. Their report vindicates every argument Labour has made against the government's massive tax breaks for oil and gas companies, under its Transferable Tax History (TTH) policy.

TTH uniquely allows companies buying North Sea oil and gas fields to inherit the tax histories of the sellers. The aim is to boost further extraction of oil and gas, when existing companies no longer can. British taxpayers will now subsidise multi-billion-pound companies in accelerating the collapse of our natural world.[2]

At the time of writing the article, Clive Lewis was shadow Treasury Minister, with responsibility for sustainable economics.

As such, his comments may be seen as partisan but he highlights one of the ways that governments support the oil and gas sector. There are endless examples of government policies, both left and right wing, which are designed to support the oil and gas sector, the nuclear sector and the automotive sector. Ideological commitment to free-market forces is advocated when it serves a particular objective, but ideology is a malleable commodity. In some situations, subsidizing green industry might be claimed to be interfering with the market, in other situations, subsidizing the oil sector might be claimed to be essential support for a valuable sector of the economy. The political response to climate change will require governments, of all political colours, to define their objectives and create policies based on the evidence, rather than use ideology to justify decisions when it suits their purpose.

Barrier 4: Public opinion

Transitioning to a sustainable society will require changes to the way that we produce and consume goods. These changes will need to be supported by social consensus, but at the present time, only a minority of people are calling for these changes, and most people would probably prefer to avoid changes to their lifestyle. As the effects of climate change become increasingly apparent, there will eventually be a realization that society has to live in sustainable ways.

The challenge for the environmental movement is to shift public opinion sooner rather than later. Fortunately, there are some signs that the public awareness is starting to increase. In the UK, over the last few years it is noticeable that the media, especially the BBC, have been giving more coverage to environmental issues. Programmes such as *Blue Planet* by David Attenborough are raising public awareness and many other programmes now address issues relating to the environment.

The way in which the media cover environmental issues has also changed. Until recently, any speaker on the BBC who discussed issues relating to the threat of climate change would be matched against a speaker who put forward an alternative view. This principle was to provide a balanced debate with alternate views being represented. However, this led to situations where one person would present scientific findings and somebody else had to be found who could come onto the programme and offer an alternative view. If the scientific community is virtually unanimous in the view that climate change threatens the future then the logical corollary is that the alternative speaker will be offering opinions *not* based on science. Fortunately, the BBC now recognizes that responsible reporting is more nuanced than simply having two opposing viewpoints.

Another factor influencing public opinion is the increasing frequency with which natural disasters feature in news reports. This is largely due to the increasing severity of these disasters and the impact that they have on economies and regions. It is interesting to note that whereas several years ago the events might have been reported in terms of the death and destruction caused, these events are now reported with a focus on the causal link to climate change. Greater coverage of environmental issues will undoubtedly help raise public awareness, especially as the style of reporting is becoming less sensationalist and more investigative.

Barrier 5: Somebody else's problem

The advanced economies have been largely insulated from the consequences of climate change and for many in the West it has been somebody else's problem. If, for example, the rains in India arrive late and the rice crop fails then the price of rice in Western supermarkets might increase, but it is unlikely to cause starvation in Europe. However, in developing countries, where many communities exist at subsistence levels, disruption to the harvest could leave many people on the edge of survival.

While climate change remains someone else's problem, the pressure for change will be muted. If there is flooding in Bangladesh, Western media may carry news reports for a couple of days, but it does not directly affect those who have no connection to Bangladesh. If flooding occurs in a town in the UK, it may affect a few hundred people, but the rest of the population can sympathize and heave a huge sigh of relief that it was not them; it's someone else's problem. However, in Bangladesh, one third of the country was underwater when extreme monsoon rains caused flooding in 2020; over 500 people died and 9.6 million were affected across Bangladesh, North India and Nepal.[3]

The sense that climate change is somebody else's problem is beginning to change as the developed world begins to experience the devastating consequences of extreme weather. Examples include:

- 2005 hurricane Katrina in New Orleans: 1,200–1,800 deaths and an estimated 400,000 people displaced.[4]
- 2012 Storm Sandy, east coast of the US: c. 150 deaths. $70 billion in damages. 20,000 people displaced one year after the event. 600,000 housing units destroyed.[5]
- 2018 forest fires in California: In excess of 215,000 acres destroyed. 44 deaths. 250,000 people evacuated.[6]
- 2020 bush fires in Australia destroyed 21 per cent of Australia's forest.[7]

Currently, the wealthy economies have the resources to adapt to the short-term effects of climate change, such as investing in flood defences for low-lying communities, but the point will come where the battle against nature is no longer winnable. While wealthy economies have the ability to manage the consequences, this will delay the pressure for change. Similarly, while only a tiny proportion of the population are directly affected, the problem can be ignored for a bit longer. For the moment, many nations are able to delude themselves that it is still someone else's problem.

Barrier 6: Scale and complexity of the problem

One of the reasons why governments might be caught like rabbits in the headlights is that the scientific data on climate change is overwhelmingly complex. Political processes work better when there are simple problems with simple solutions; policies are easier to formulate, proposals are easier to explain and actions are easier to implement. When problems are highly complex and things are poorly understood it might be easier to offer spurious information that distracts from the real issues and delay action on the basis that there is insufficient evidence or that scientific opinions differ.

Although the scientific community is overwhelmingly in agreement that climate change poses a real and significant threat, there are still differing views as to how quickly temperatures will rise and how serious the consequences are likely to be. Even though the range of likely outcomes all result in catastrophic outcome for civilization, the fact that there is a variance of how quickly we might be overtaken by disaster can be taken as a reason to cast doubt on the scientific evidence.

On the other hand, economists can offer forecasts to predict how the global economy might be impacted by events such as the rapid decline in the oil sector or a contraction in global trade. These forecasts may or may not be accurate, but there is a sense that we understand the assumptions and we can control the data that is entered into such economic models. Therefore, politicians might feel more comfortable heeding the warnings of economists and business strategists that warn against drastic changes to our economy than they do listening to the warnings of climate scientists. It would be tragic if politicians delay action on climate change because we prefer to be guided by the reassurance of economic modelling rather than scientific evidence. We cannot prevaricate while we review all the scientific data, evaluate every different scenario and quantify just how serious it will be. The data may be complex and the implications unquantifiable, but we know enough to place the environment as our overriding priority.

Barrier 7: Capacity to deliver

When an organization undergoes a process of change there are a number of activities that need to be managed. Typically, these will include:

- Raising awareness of the need to change.
- Building executive commitment.
- Developing the strategy and plan.
- Engaging stakeholders.
- Securing funding for resources.

- Establishing a highly skilled team.
- Initiating programme governance.
- Initiating a programme of work.
- Managing a programme of change.
- Embedding and sustaining the changes.

If the process of organizational change is analogous to socio-economic change then we are barely at the stage of *awareness of the need to change*. Each one of these stages requires a specific set of competencies and commitment of resources. Currently, we lack the capacity to manage a process that enables even the first stage to be met. It is questionable whether we have the capacity to deliver the other stages successfully.

Barrier 8: International isolationism

The transition from fossil fuels to renewables will create winners and losers. The nations that are *winners* will need to support the *losers* through a period of economic transition. Without such support, the oil exporting nations will pursue policies of self-interest rather than abandon the source of their wealth and influence. This commitment to long-term international collaborating will require an acknowledgement that self-interest is not best served by policies of isolationism. In recent decades, many of the most powerful nations have pursued foreign policies that sought to protect their interests. Although this appears to be the de facto approach to foreign policy, it has not always been this way. One of the major initiatives in post-war foreign policy was the Marshall Plan, which funded the reconstruction of Germany after 1945. This was an outstanding example of winners supporting losers.

The US provided approximately $12 billion (more than $120 billion at 2020 valuations) to western Europe, particularly West Germany, to ensure that mainland Europe would not sink into depression and, thereby, once again create the political conditions that might allow extremist parties to gain support. The particular fear after 1945 was the expansion of communism. A more recent example of winners supporting losers has been the reunification of Germany when the West German economy funded the economic regeneration of East Germany. This process had significant negative economic consequences in the short term, but there was a sense of shared purpose among many Germans who wanted to see the country reunited again. Behind both of these examples is the realization that the interests of the donor are protected by funding the cost of social and economic transition.

Barrier 9: The economic cost

It is inevitable that there will be a significant cost to societal transition, but that is not a reason for delay. There have been many examples of societies confronting threats to their survival, and history tells us that a successful outcome requires action that is appropriate to the scale of the challenge, not a response that is determined by concerns of cost. Churchill's response to Hitler was not dependent on how much the war might cost. Similarly, we cannot delay action on climate change because the economic costs are high.

Barrier 10: Failure to acknowledge the inevitable

Ultimately, even if we ignore the problems of climate change, the current economic model has to undergo a radical transformation. Global populations are growing fast, the demand for energy is increasing, carbon-based energy sources are declining and energy prices will inevitably increase. Carbon-based energy cannot supply our needs indefinitely. Unless we eliminate our dependency on fossil fuels, the energy crisis will create poverty, social unrest, regional conflict and lead to the collapse of the global economy. Even without the threat of global warming, we would have change the way that we live.

It is difficult to find reasons to be cheerful when one considers the scale of the challenge, the consequences of failure and the low probability that civilization will address the problems successfully. The optimists and idealists may hold out hope that human nature is intrinsically good, that the nations of the world will come together to achieve common purpose and that the threat of catastrophe will be averted.

The pessimists and the pragmatists, on the other hand, may point to the sorry history of humanity that has endless examples of stupidity, tragedy and the ultimate demise of civilizations that failed to acknowledge the threats confronting them. They may hold little hope that the human race is capable of rising above personal or political aspirations in order to create a new tomorrow. Instead, they may feel that in times of trouble all we can do is to protect the things we hold most dear and fight to survive in a dangerous world.

Whether the optimists or pessimists are ultimately proved right, in times of crisis it is important to remain optimistic. Most importantly, we need our political and corporate leaders to believe that the situation is redeemable; otherwise, they might seek to defend their power and wealth in order to protect themselves against the inevitable consequences of environmental collapse.

10

Perceptions and Reality

Chapter summary

This chapter considers how we perceive our situation and our ability to ignore problems that are about to overwhelm us. This affects the way that we respond to potential threats and our ability to reassure ourselves that we are taking appropriate action. It looks at the need to acknowledge the threats facing humanity, the need for a collective epiphany and considers whether humanity has the capacity for collective action or whether we will become increasingly isolationist.

Introduction

It is amazing that the human race has survived for so long. It is even more amazing that the first humans ever managed to survive their emergence in the vast bushlands of East Africa; they didn't have the strength to fight off large predators; they couldn't run very fast; they didn't even breed very fast. Perhaps, part of the explanation lies in the human ability to assess a situation and develop an appropriate response. Our early survival decisions were *fight or flight* decisions. These days the decisions are more complex. The threats we face are of a bigger magnitude than a marauding lion.

The task of determining an appropriate survival response is ever more difficult. Whether we have the ability to take effective action against the multitude of threats that currently face humanity remains to be seen. Presumably, there will come some point when we no longer have the capacity to assimilate all the relevant information and implement an effective response. Maybe we have reached a point where the scale of the threat will overwhelm us. Perhaps we are deluding ourselves that we are still in control. Arguably, our biggest challenge is to acknowledge the reality of the threat now facing humanity. We need to face up to this rather than burying our heads in the sand and hoping it will be all right.

Changing perceptions

This book has argued that radical social and economic change is required. Whether people wish to change will depend on their perceptions of the future compared to the present. For example, if levels of positivity or negativity were measured on a scale of +5 (positive) to −5 (negative), then it is possible to plot how people feel about the impact of change over time.

Figure 10.1: Perceptions of the impact of change

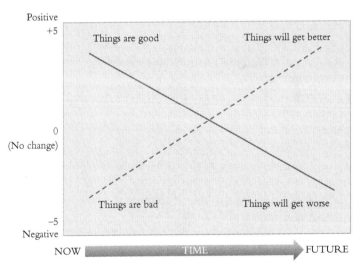

Source: Unattributable

The difficulty with seeking electoral support for policies to address climate change is that many people may feel that things are *good*, in the sense that society does not face serious threats. If people feel that changes will result in changes that they *don't want*, then their perceptions of the future will be *bad*. In Figure 10.1, the solid line represents this perception of change from NOW to FUTURE.

In order to build support for action on climate change it will be necessary to raise awareness that the current situation is *bad* (unsustainable) and it is only by undergoing change that we can make the situation *good* (sustainable).

Those people that feel that the situation NOW is *good* will need to revise their perceptions before they support changes. In other words, their perception of the current state of the world will need to switch to *bad*. At the same time, it will be necessary to build a *positive* vision for the FUTURE. In Figure 10.1, the dotted line represents this perception of NOW to FUTURE.

Acknowledging threats

Human nature has a tendency to wait until a situation becomes serious before responding to a threat. At a trivial level, as individuals, we might delay completing a tax return (although we know it has to be done), paying credit card bills or stopping to fill the car with fuel. There is a sense of: *I don't want to do it. It can wait a bit longer.* It is not difficult to justify prevarication over relatively minor issues but this tendency to avoid impending problems can have serious implications in other situations. Even when confronted by life-or-death situations people usually need clear evidence of the alternative outcomes presented before taking action. Examples from history include:

- Pompeii: It appears that there was time to escape after the first stages of the eruption had started but many people remained in Pompeii. It was about eight hours before pyroclastic blasts caused the death of those in the surrounding area. There appears to have been more than sufficient time to escape but the citizens of Pompeii seemed to have decided that the situation was not too serious. Maybe they had become used to minor volcanic activity and dismissed the potential threat. Whatever the reason, they had time to get away, but they misjudged the risk that they faced.

- Titanic: Passengers and crew believed that the ship was unsinkable and there were long delays before the lifeboats were launched. Even after it was clear that the ship was sinking, the captain appears never to have given a formal order for the ship to be abandoned.

There is a behavioural trait that leads people to prefer the current (known) situation rather than move to an alternative (unknown) situation. This preference for the known rather than the unknown exists even when there is overwhelming evidence that change is urgently required. Reasons for this might include:

- Denial of the facts: *Things can't really be that bad.*
- Sense of inevitability: *If it is going to happen then there is not much that I can do about it.*
- It won't affect me: *It might happen, but it will affect other people and I will be all right.*
- I will watch to see what other people do: *I don't want to be seen as the first person to panic.*
- Rabbit in the headlights: *I'm confused. I probably ought to do something, but I don't know what.*

These characteristics of human nature can result in collective inertia, causing delays at a time when a rapid response is required. There will be situations where this trait brings certain benefits, as without it we would be like meerkats, constantly scuttling about, avoiding potential threats. However, there is the risk that even when the evidence of impending disaster is clear, people are likely to perform mental gymnastics to convince themselves that the situation cannot really be as terrifyingly bad as the evidence implies. There will be some people who deny the evidence, even when it is unambiguously presented. There will be others that convince themselves that it will not affect them directly. There will be some that believe the threat but feel unable to do anything about it. Others will ignore threats when they encounter situations that they neither understand nor control.

These psychological processes will operate in situations where the need for change is clear and unambiguous, so it is not surprising that we are resistant to change when there is uncertainty or doubt. The ability to sow the seeds of confusion is one of the reasons that the climate denial lobbyists have been so successful. They only need to suggest that the evidence on global warming is flawed and people will use this perceived uncertainty as the justification to push their concerns to the back of their minds. Conversely, those seeking to raise awareness about the threat of climate change will struggle to raise a response, even when the scientific evidence is overwhelming.

In recent years, there has been much attention given to the phenomenon of *fake news.* This is nothing new. Throughout history, there have been politicians, emperors and snake-oil sellers that have made statements they know to be false but which serve their purpose. The problem we face in the 21st century is that social media now provides a vehicle to disseminate ideas to huge numbers of people. Given our natural response to believe information that fits our individual paradigms, the deluge of information is continually filtered by our subconscious so that we pick out the information we want to hear, in effect reinforcing our own prejudices.

Even if the scientific evidence starts to change perceptions, it will require more than an intellectual acceptance of scientific information before people demand action on climate change; it will require an *emotional* transformation. For some people this might happen as a result of seeing a documentary, such as *An Inconvenient Truth,* a film about ex-Vice President Al Gore's efforts to raise awareness of the causes and impending consequences of climate change.

Alternatively, it might be an event that affects people directly, such as a drought, that destroys their farm, or a forest fire that burns their home. For other people their attitudes might gradually be changed by a slow drip feed of information. Whatever the process, ultimately it requires an emotional shift where previous beliefs are challenged and then reformed. This process of shifting values, attitudes and behaviours will ultimately require some kind of epiphany. In other words, individuals and communities need to undergo an experience that affects them at an *emotional* level, rather than attempting to change attitudes by presenting *evidence.*

From epiphany to action

The transition from epiphany to action consists of two stages: acknowledgement of the need to change and implementing an appropriate response.

1. Acknowledgement of the need for change.
   The first step in a process of change is acknowledgement that change is necessary, either to avoid a problem or to exploit an opportunity. Survival and growth, whether for organisms, plants, organizations or communities, requires sensitivity to the external environment and the ability to assess the threat (or opportunity). As discussed above, there may be many reasons why humans fail to acknowledge an impending threat.
2. Implementing an appropriate response.
   It is necessary to determine an appropriate response, once the threat has been recognized and assessed. This requires some mechanism to weigh options and outcomes so that action can be taken. One of the problems in determining an appropriate response to climate change is that most of us lack the capability to assess the complexity of the information available.

There is a risk that action is delayed while we seek to understand the multitude of interdependencies, implications and potential scenarios. This complexity strains our capability to assimilate information and define the optimum response. This is certainly the case with the scientific evidence relating to climate change; however, while the science is complex the problem is simple. We know that CO_2 emissions have to be reduced and we understand the major factors causing the increase in CO_2. At its most simple, we have to stop emitting CO_2 into the atmosphere. It logically follows that we have to transition from an economic model that is based on fossil fuels.

Integrity and transparency

The public debate on climate change needs to be underpinned by transparency of the decision-making processes to ensure impartiality in the way that evidence is collated, analyzed and interpreted. In some countries, such as the US, the power of lobbyists is deeply entrenched. In Europe and other advanced economies, it may be less overt, but they still have a significant impact on policy. It is important that strategy and policy are based on evidence and objective assessment, but this will only happen if policy is based on independent, specialist advice.

Failure to ensure integrity and transparency of the scientific evidence will result in confusion and cause delays in implementing effective action. An example of this is when the University of East Anglia was accused of distorting scientific evidence. In 2009, hackers gained access to thousands of emails relating to the activities of the Climate Research Unit, University of East Anglia. This appears to have been part of a deliberate attempt to discredit the climate science.[1]

Among the thousands of emails that were hacked, there was one written by a member of the Climate Research Unit that suggested certain data relating to changes in global temperatures should be ignored as it presented a confusing set of results. While one set of data showed global temperatures were rising rapidly, another set of data showed that there was little evidence of global warming. One of the researchers suggested that the data showing little sign of global warming should be discounted.

On the face of it, this sounds as though data is being manipulated, but the reasons for discounting some of the information need to be understood. The following points offer a brief summary of the reasons behind the proposal to discount part of the data.

- During the early 1700s until the early 1800s, scientists started taking the first measurements of atmospheric temperatures in several different parts of the world.
- These measurements were taken with thermometers.
- Prior to the 1700s, there were no detailed scientific records on global temperatures, as the thermometer was not invented until 1714.
- From the 1800s onwards, these measurements became more widespread and tracked atmospheric temperatures in a wide range of locations around the world.

- Attempts to measure global temperatures during the millennia prior to 1800 had been undertaken by other evidence, including measuring periods of fast or slow tree growth, achieved by examining the width of tree rings in prehistoric samples.
- This meant that there were two different methodologies for measuring global temperatures; scientifically *accurate* methods using thermometers and scientifically *estimated* methods, primarily based on measuring tree rings.
- When the method of measuring tree rings was used to estimate global temperatures in the period from the 1960s onwards, it implied that there was little evidence of global warming (cooler weather, less growth, rings closer together).
- If the two sets of data (tree ring data and thermometer measurements) were compared it showed contradictory results.
- The tree ring data showing less growth post 1960 was due to factors other than atmospheric temperature, for example, high levels of pollution, acid rain and other factors associated with the impact of human activity.
- Thermometers offer an accurate method of measuring atmospheric temperatures, whereas tree ring measurements only offer an estimation and show a trend over time.
- Evidence based on tree ring measurements from 1960 was less reliable and this was the reason that data after 1960 was excluded from a specific set of charts that were being presented by the University of East Anglia.

Reports in the media failed to explain the reason for excluding misleading data and instead, repeated the claims made by the hackers that scientists had manipulated evidence on climate change. Unfortunately, the consequences of this event damaged the reputation of the Climate Research Unit, one of the leading institutions in climate science research and the fall-out from the scandal derailed negotiations at the 2009 Copenhagen Climate Change Summit. When this story hit the headlines, it created confusion among the public and gave a window of opportunity to those that sought to discredit the overwhelming scientific consensus.

Our ability to address the threat of climate change will depend on the information that is available to us and our response to the information. If the information is distorted, if evidence is denied or if we stick our heads in the sand and refuse to accept the risks that we face then we are unlikely to survive. In the early stages of human evolution, we were highly effective at banding together in small groups to protect ourselves from dangerous predators. Whether we are able to use our collective abilities to unite against a new threat waits to be seen. But one thing is clear; collaboration will be critical.

International collaboration

In a globally connected economy, it is self-evident that international cooperation is required. Issues to be addressed will include:

Commitment to total global carbon emissions

This point has been discussed previously but it is worth stressing that even now, after all the efforts of the UN to secure agreement through the Conference of the Parties, we do not have this most basic precondition to controlling global warming.

Managing a just transition

The international community will need to reach agreement on mechanisms to support national economies that currently depend upon fossil fuels. It will also need to address the risk that some communities will benefit from the new wealth and opportunities created by an economic transition, whilst others might find themselves excluded, creating conditions that could create a new wealth gap in society.

Environmental costing

There will need to be international agreement on methods of environmental costing so that international supply chains, production processes and market pricing take account of environmental costs.

Reform of global financial markets

One of the core concepts within The Green New Deal is the reform of the financial markets. In essence, the capital markets need to serve the needs of society, not the other way around. The financial markets are so powerful that they have little accountability to governments or society. The ability of banks to create virtually unlimited credit drives consumption and causes the unlimited exploitation of natural resources. This is good for banks. It is less good for the planet.[2]

Developing the required capabilities

The transition will require every facet of society to build new capabilities. Some examples are illustrated here:

- Leadership capabilities to define and communicate the vision, objectives and goals that will achieve the required social and economic change.
- Political capabilities to implement the vision, set a clear strategy and design policies to guide the economic transition;
- Technical capabilities to develop the infrastructure to support a zero-carbon economy.
- Organizational capabilities to manage disruption to existing industries, and manage the transition of skills/resources to new economic activity.
- Financial capabilities to mobilize resources and allocate capital to new social and economic programmes.

The goal of net zero

At present, the projections for reducing carbon emissions show that it is virtually impossible to achieve zero-carbon without radical change to the global economy. For example, industries such as aviation, steel and cement are major carbon emitters and it will require fundamental changes to these industries if emission levels are to be reduced. Similarly, agriculture is a major emitter of greenhouse gases, largely attributable to the production of chemical fertilizers and large-scale animal farming. A meaningful reduction in greenhouse gases would require both changes to farming practices and a significant decline in the demand of beef and other animal products. Because there is a wide gap between what is considered feasible (technically, politically and economically), the concept of *net zero* has been adopted as a means of bridging the gap between the total elimination of fossil fuels and the reality that we cannot eliminate them completely; some form of carbon offset is required.

The concept of net zero means that countries can continue to generate greenhouse gases but then offset these emissions by activities such as planting trees or other mechanisms to recover CO_2 from the atmosphere. This mechanism of achieving net zero is appealing as it allows carbon emissions to continue while being justified on the basis that a compensating activity will absorb the carbon. However, there are a number of problems with relying on net zero as the route to prevent global warming. First, the mechanisms for offsetting may not offer a genuine like-for-like carbon offset. Second, carbon offsetting may divert attention from implementing the changes that are required, allowing carbon emission to continue to increase. Third, some schemes for offsetting may be of dubious quality with exaggerated claims of benefits that in reality do little to recover carbon from the atmosphere.

However, even if there are effective mechanisms to achieve carbon offsetting we still face the problem that the rate at which forests are being destroyed will probably exceed the rate at which trees are being planted. This will mean that carbon emissions continue to rise, yet we delude ourselves that we are addressing the problem by planting trees.

There is little doubt that effective carbon offsetting will become an essential part of the response to climate change, but it is important that it does not become a substitute for implementing the transformation that is required. Carbon offsetting provides emergency triage, rather than a cure for global warming. Taking action to recover landscapes, forests and reverse desertification should be happening in any case, not being implemented simply as a mechanism for carbon offset.

Green alchemy

In the past, many companies have engaged in some form of *green washing* as they attempted to present themselves as environmentally responsible. There is a risk that we may enter a new age of corporate smoke and mirrors as corporate marketing seeks to convince consumers of their green credentials. For example, there is a risk that airlines might start to claim that their flights will be green because they will be burning kerosene that has been produced from waste; methane that would have gone into the atmosphere will be used to produce a new type of kerosene. However, the fact remains that every flight will continue to emit greenhouse gases into the atmosphere. Global warming will continue to increase. We should be looking at ways to eliminate greenhouse gas emissions, not trying to find new ways of recycling them into the atmosphere. Yes, of course, capturing methane to produce aviation fuel will reduce the need to extract oil from the ground and convert it into kerosene, but it is not environmentally friendly flying. We could end up with a situation where there is no incentive to reduce waste, because it has value as aviation fuel, and there is no perceived need to reduce emissions from aviation because it is proclaimed to be *green*.

Green politics

Green political parties have largely failed to attract significant levels of support. While there are some exceptions such as Germany, Denmark and the Scandinavian countries, in most countries, the green parties hold little power or influence. The failure of green parties to attract significant support probably reflects that most societies continue to prioritize economic growth, wealth and low taxes, over concerns for the environment.

At some point, the reality of the impending disaster will penetrate the public consciousness and there will inevitably be a reaction. The changes that are required in our social and economic systems will require the understanding and support of all those affected, requiring stakeholder engagement on an unprecedented scale. It is essential that populations understand the current trajectory, the implications for their future and the need for change. Political parties cannot continue to make empty claims about their environmental credentials while covertly protecting the interests of organizations that damage the planet.

It is essential that the electorate develops greater understanding and becomes motivated to demand action to reverse the rise in CO_2 emissions. Political strategies to reverse climate change will only become a reality when the demands of an informed electorate outweigh pressure from the corporate lobbyists. Politicians that fail to respond to the demands of the electorate will be out of power and therefore of no further use to the vested interests. A smooth transition requires the political establishment to engage with the environmental campaigners, not reject them.

The economic crash in 2008 precipitated problems for many in the advanced economies. Large numbers of people who previously held secure, middle-class jobs or skilled work are now in lower-skilled and less fulfilling work. A growing proportion is on part-time or non-contract work. While various Western governments proclaim that employment levels are high, this data disguises a deterioration in the quality of life for many people. There is a simmering anger and a sense that people are *not being heard*. This is opening the door to political leaders offering simplistic solutions to a brighter future.

We have already seen how distrust of the establishment resulted in the Brexit vote in the UK and Trump's election in 2016. Yet, there is little room for optimism that anti-establishment responses offer solutions to the social or economic problems that affect many people's lives. Indeed, restrictions to trade, public spending reductions and isolationist policies are only going to exacerbate the problems facing many people. Anger and frustration are likely to grow, accompanied by increasing social unrest. All of these problems will divert attention away from concerns for global warming.

Heading towards social collapse

We will soon reach a point where the planet's resources will be unable to support continual growth. This will have significant implications, not just for the global economy but also for the values and beliefs that underpin our social structures. Social attitudes will be fundamentally challenged as our current socio-economic model is shown to be a fallacy. The collective hopes of humanity for a happy and prosperous future will be replaced by fears of poverty, hardship and the eventual collapse of human society. There will be anger at the deception that has been perpetrated by politicians and corporate organizations for pursuing short-term gains while continuing to ignore the evidence that had been building for the last 50 years. The sight of the wealthy elite pulling up the drawbridge and using their power to assure their own survival will only heighten this sense of betrayal.

The foundations of modern industrial society will collapse, the principles that underpinned an international global economy will be invalidated and the forces that bind society through the concept of a social contract will be eroded as the legitimacy of governments and corporations falls into disrepute. It is difficult to predict how governments will cope with this new reality, but it is likely that there will be a growing shift towards protectionism, national self-interest and increasingly oppressive authoritarian rule.

One of the major consequences of social and economic collapse will be that it becomes increasingly difficult to reach national and international consensus on a coordinated response to climate change. Not only will the natural environment become locked in a feedback loop where global warming triggers events that further increase global temperatures, but also society and the economy will be locked in a feedback loop where social collapse triggers factors that cause rising distrust and greater isolationism.

If we are to overcome the challenge of global warming, it will be essential to maintain confidence in the political establishment. Those in power will need to secure their legitimacy by demonstrating that they have the desire and capability to protect the natural environment for the benefit of all members of society.

PART III

The Call to Action

Introduction

Part III of this book considers the actions that we need to take, individually and collectively, in order to reverse climate change. For the last few decades, there has been a general awareness that climate change is a problem, but it is only in the last few years that the scale of the threat has grown within the public consciousness. In his speech to the World Economic Forum in 2019, Sir David Attenborough made a number of key points, including:[1]

- If people truly understand what is at stake, they will give permission to governments to get on with the practical solutions.
- We need a plan and apply ourselves to the problem.
- What we do now and in the next few years will profoundly affect the next few thousand years.

It might be hoped that, to quote Sir David, 'if people truly understood what is at stake' then governments would be empowered, and indeed pressurized, into taking the actions required. However, many governments seem to be more concerned with protecting the status quo than initiating change. In addition, getting people to truly understand what is at stake is difficult, as human nature frequently prefers to ignore unpleasant realities. The second point, 'we need a plan' is at the heart of the problem and, at present, there is still little evidence that such a plan exists.

Any plan would need to be implemented under the appropriate authority to ensure effective international cooperation and governance. For this to happen there would need to be a radical change in the way that the UN operates and the authority that it exerts. Whether or not this might be achieved, is debatable.

Most importantly, there needs to be intergovernmental consensus on what a future world might look like; we need a clear and united vision for our global society. Achieving consensus among nearly 200 countries will be difficult, especially if some of the key players are reluctant to acknowledge that climate change is even a problem.

In 2019, Sir David Attenborough highlighted the urgency of our situation by stressing that: 'Unless we sort ourselves out in the next decade or so we are dooming our children and our grandchildren to an appalling future.'

Sir David's message is clear; we have only a few years left in which we can address the threat of climate change. If we are lucky, we will be able to apply new technologies effectively, change consumer behaviour and prevent the worst scenarios associated with runaway global warming. If we are very, very lucky, we may evolve into a better civilization.

11

The Great Transition

Chapter summary

This chapter considers the process of transition from both a political perspective and a technical perspective. The political perspective starts with an appraisal of three alternative scenarios for civilization and goes on to consider the types of policies that will be required if the current economic model is to become sustainable. The technical perspective offers a very brief summary of some of the technological changes that will support the rapid transition to a sustainable society.

Political transition

History teaches us that civilizations grow, flourish and then decline. The Aztecs, the Roman Empire, Chinese dynasties, the Mongol empire and the trading empires of various European countries have all dominated regions of the world for a while and then declined. The challenge facing our modern global civilization is that unless we evolve to a sustainable society we not only risk the collapse of our modern civilization but we jeopardize the survival of humanity.

Over the next few years, we need to address six primary factors that will determine the future of humanity:

- Population.
- Economy.
- Environment.

- Equity/society.
- Technology.
- Conflict.

These factors were identified in a book, *The Great Transition: The Promise and Lure of the Times Ahead*, by Paul Raskin et al (2002).[1] The book considers whether it is possible to achieve the *Great Transition* and if not, what alternative futures might be in store for us. It offers three scenarios and examines how the aforementioned six factors will be affected according to different outcomes. The three scenarios identified by Raskin et al are:

1. Conventional worlds – characterized by
   - Market forces: Self-correcting logic of market forces.
   - Policy reform: Government intervention to support a sustainable future.
2. Barbarization – characterized by
   - Breakdown: Conflict and crisis spiral into total collapse.
   - Fortress world: Authoritarian response creating a global apartheid of elite minority and impoverished majority.
3. Great transitions – characterized by
   - Eco-communalism: Self-sufficiency, localized models of social, economic and democratic activity.
   - New sustainability paradigm: Global society, cultural cross-fertilization, economic connectedness based on environmentally sustainable values.

It is possible that several of these scenarios will be enacted simultaneously in different political or geographical regions of the world. For example, the US might pursue the *conventional worlds* scenario, relying on market forces to encourage new sustainable technologies, although the rate of adoption might be slow due to continued availability of cheap alternatives. At the same time, the EU might pursue radical *policy reform* to manage a transition to renewable energy and the adoption of other new, sustainable, technologies. Meanwhile, there may be other countries that move towards *Barbarization* as declining harvests, poverty and deprivation lead to social unrest, riots and regional conflict.

In the short to medium term, say 10–20 years, these various scenarios may exist as a set of alternative road maps, describing how individual countries or regions respond to the impacts of climate change. Ultimately, however, unless there is the *great transition*, the various alternative scenarios will move towards the same end point and descend into *breakdown* and *fortress world*.

Figure 11.1: Transition scenarios

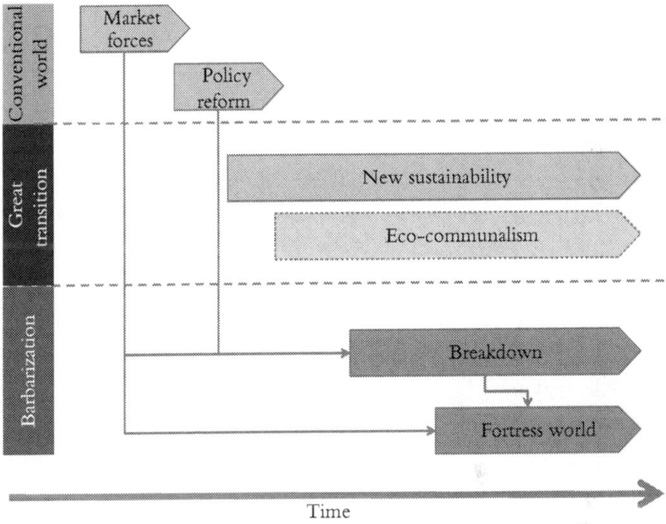

Source: Richard Joy, based on the concepts of Paul Raskin et al.

Figure 11.1 illustrates that, in the long-term, market forces will fail to achieve the necessary social and economic transition and will, ultimately, lead to *breakdown* and *fortress world*. Policy reform may be able to delay the collapse into *breakdown* and *fortress world*, but *policy reform* will only delay the inevitable. Figure 11.1 shows that the *conventional worlds* model will eventually slip into *Barbarization* unless there is a fundamental change in our socio-economic model that is represented by *great transitions*.

Collapse of the *conventional world*

Much of this book has discussed the proposition that market forces will not, on their own, provide solutions to reverse global warming. Even policy reform, on its own, will not achieve the fundamental changes that are required. To quote Raskin et al:

> **Policy Reform** is the realm of necessity – it seeks to minimize environmental and social disruption, while the quality of life remains unexamined. The new sustainability paradigm transcends reform to ask anew the question that Socrates posed long ago: how shall we live? This is the **Great Transitions** path, the realm of desirability.

The transition to a sustainable society will require the *great transition* that delivers potential scenarios described as the *new sustainability paradigm*, and *eco-communalism*. The concept of the *new sustainability paradigm* is based on the idea of revising the concept of progress. Civilization has now reached a point where, for many people, their reasonable aspirations of personal fulfilment can be satisfied and the level of consumption is more than adequate for their needs. The problems facing the poor in the world, poverty, hunger and disease, are largely due to the failure to ensure an equitable distribution of wealth rather than constraints on the planet's resources. If we stopped allocating a third of our fertile lands to the feeding of livestock and moved to a low meat, low dairy diet we would be better able to feed the global population in ways that are sustainable. If we revised our current lifestyles characterized by high consumption and rapid disposal, then we would create the opportunity for human civilization to live within the environmental constraints of the planet. As stated in Raskin et al:

> The vision of a better life can turn to non-material dimensions of fulfilment – the quality of life, the quality of human solidarity and the quality of the earth. With the Keynes (1972), we can dream of a time when 'we shall once more value ends above means and prefer the good to the useful'.

The concept of *eco-communalism* arises from views associated with the reaction to the industrial world by the 19th century utopians and the *Small is Beautiful* philosophy of E.F. Schumacher.[2] This was a landmark book in the environmental movement and questioned the rationale of mega-organizations and the pursuit of economies of scale. Schumacher considered whether the economic benefits justified the negative consequences for the environment and the social impact of low-wage, repetitive work. The book preceded the phenomenon of globalization but anticipated the consequences of a globalized economy. Published in 1973, his ideas set the groundwork for many of the ideas that underpin the current environmental movement, such as the principle that organizations should focus on *purpose*, not simply profit.

The road to barbarism

The term *barbarism* describes the collapse of an ordered society. Over the next few decades, the effects of climate change will cause serious disruption to regions such as Africa, Asia and the Middle East. Large proportions of their populations already have little resilience to the challenges that are to come and they will increasingly suffer drought, starvation and civil unrest. This social and economic breakdown will trigger political turmoil and mass migration that will have an impact on other regions of the world that had, thus far, avoided the worst consequences of global warming. A likely outcome will be that the Western world will adopt a *fortress world* response in order to avoid being overwhelmed by the pressure of destitute refugees. This might avoid mass migration into the wealthier countries, but growing regional chaos will disrupt trade, food supplies and the supply of raw materials. Those countries that had hoped that they could use their wealth to mitigate the effects of global warming will eventually realize that they are unable to insulate themselves from the consequences of climate change.

Another assessment of possible scenarios has been succinctly summarized by Rupert Read, Associate Professor of Philosophy at the University of East Anglia, and environmental campaigner (and key figure within Extinction Rebellion). The following quotation is taken from a book by Samuel Alexandra and Rupert

Read, *This Civilisation is Finished*. The exert is quoted in an article that appeared in *Resliance.org*.[3] He states:

> As I see things, there are three broad possible futures that lie ahead:
> - This civilisation could collapse utterly and terminally, as a result of climatic instability (leading for instance to catastrophic food shortages as a probable mechanism of collapse), or possibly sooner than that, through nuclear war, pandemic, or financial collapse leading to mass civil breakdown. Any of these are likely to be precipitated in part by ecological/climate instability, as Darfur and Syria were. Or
> - This civilisation (we) will manage to seed a future successor-civilisation(s), as this one collapses. Or
> - This civilisation will somehow manage to transform itself deliberately, radically and rapidly, in an unprecedented manner, in time to avert collapse.

The first two scenarios describe the collapse of civilization, and the third scenario holds out hope that somehow civilization may transform itself before it is too late. His premise is that whichever way you look at it, our current civilization has to undergo transition or it is ultimately finished.

The challenge that we face is managing the various stages in a process of transition. We cannot move from the current globalized, free-market economy that is driven by corporate power, the financial markets and the ideologies of national governments, to a utopian state of universal happiness and environmental sustainability. There will be a series of stages in the process of transition rather than a single leap into a new world.

The immediate priority is to slow the rate of global warming so that we have sufficient time to manage a process of transition. This will require government intervention and a strategy to influence *market forces* and manage *policy reform*, but this only provides a stepping stone to transition and should not be seen as an end in itself.

This government intervention will cause shifts in consumer behaviour and support gradual changes to attitudes and societal norms. These cultural changes will start to reinforce consumer behaviour and support a growing understanding of why changes are required.

Technology transition

The past couple of decades have seen huge advances in sustainable technologies. The pace of this change has been remarkable. Some technologies are now well established, such as wind turbines, but there are other technologies that have yet to become established but will have an important part to play in a sustainable society. Some of the required technologies already exist, although they may not be commercially established. There are other areas where practical solutions have not yet been developed.

This section is not intended as a comprehensive list of all the innovations that will be needed for a sustainable society, it is simply intended to indicate a few of the key areas where technology will enable society to retain the benefits that have been enjoyed in the past but in ways that are sustainable.

There are four areas for technical innovation that have been identified in this section:

- Hydrogen/ammonia.
- Concrete.
- Refrigerants.
- Aircraft engines.

Hydrogen/ammonia

The role of hydrogen is not yet widely established but it would seem inevitable that it has a significant role to play. The advantages of hydrogen are that it provides a high amount of energy in a relatively small volume (as a compressed gas). The energy in 1 kg of hydrogen is similar to the energy in 1 gallon of petrol. The disadvantages of hydrogen are that it requires specialist equipment to handle it in the compressed form. In addition, it normally requires some chemical reaction to produce and this can be energy intensive in itself. Therefore, hydrogen production is worthwhile where there are readily available forms of cheap, renewable energy. For example, hydrogen production plants could be integrated into the energy grid so that when there is excess renewable energy (eg the wind blows at night when there is little energy demand), it could be converted to hydrogen. The difficulty with this is that hydrogen production plants are generally designed to run for consistent periods, not switch off and on. Although this type of application is already in use, there are limitations. However, the greater opportunity is to produce hydrogen in places where energy is consistently available, such as solar farms in hot dry regions close to the equator. The problem is that shipping hydrogen as a compressed gas is expensive. The solution is to produce ammonia, a product that can be readily converted to hydrogen.[4]

One advantage of using ammonia is that the technology and infrastructure for transporting and handling ammonia already exists. Therefore, ammonia can be produced cheaply in areas such as North Africa and the Middle East, shipped to global destinations and then converted to hydrogen where it would be distributed for use in applications such as cars, vans, trains and ships.

Concrete

The production of concrete creates huge amounts of greenhouse gas, partly because the process requires significant energy but also because the production process produces CO_2. An article in *Carbon Brief* gives an excellent summary of the environmental impact of the concrete industry.

> If the cement industry were a country, it would be the third largest emitter of CO_2 in the world.

> In 2015, it generated around 2.8bn tonnes of CO_2, equivalent to 8% of the global total – a greater share than any country other than China or the US.

> Cement use is set to rise as global urbanisation and economic development increases demand for new buildings and infrastructure.[5]

The impact of emissions will be reduced as producers switch to renewable sources of energy and this has the potential to reduce emissions by 50 per cent. The hope is that other raw materials will be found to replace the limestone/clay mix that is currently used. Alternative materials are available, such as fly ash and blast furnace slag, but although this will reduce the emissions, these materials are the product of other processes that produce carbon emissions so they are not a complete solution. Other options that are being investigated include the addition of graphene, which greatly enhances the strength of the material, meaning that less quantity is required for any given application.

The introduction of new types of construction may lead to less concrete being used in the construction process. For example, modular building construction might favour buildings that use steel, wood and brick rather than concrete. The search for practical alternatives to concrete is the subject of much research but practical alternatives are not yet commercially available. Further innovation in this area will be required if we are to reduce the environmental damage of construction industry.

Refrigerants

The environmental damage of refrigerants hit the headlines in the 1980s when the damage to the ozone became widely publicized. The 1987 Montreal Protocol was an international agreement to stop emitting CFC and HCFC. This agreement has been effective in reversing the damage to the ozone but the chemicals that have replaced them, hydrofluorocarbons, while not damaging to the ozone, do contribute to climate change. To quote from *Drawdown* (editor Paul Hawkin, 2017): '... (HFCs) have no deleterious effect on the ozone layer, but their capacity to warm the atmosphere is one thousand to nine thousand times greater than that of carbon dioxide...'[6]

Drawdown identifies refrigerants as the single greatest opportunity to reduce the impact of global warming. This is based on an assessment of the potential adverse impact if it is not addressed, balanced against the cost and feasibility of taking action. Refrigerants are used widely, both domestically and commercially in fridges, air conditioning units and any application for absorbing/releasing heat. As global temperatures rise, as the global population rises, as the numbers living in urban accommodation increases, the demand for refrigerants will increase.

The release of refrigerants into the atmosphere occurs at all stages of the product lifecycle: filling, servicing, leaks due to use and disposal. It is particularly at end of life that emissions occur. Without effective regulation and control, this presents a huge environmental threat. Fortunately, it is relatively easy either to reuse gases or to process waste gas into alternative useable forms that do not present an environmental threat.

Aircraft engines

One of the conundrums for environmentalists is that there are few quick or cheap green alternatives to long-distance air travel; mostly it's a choice of fly or don't fly. Electric flight is possible but it is only practical on small aircraft for short distances. However, there are emerging technologies that use ammonia/hydrogen to create the combustive forces normally provide by jet fuel. Using engines that are similar to modern jet engines, effectively with a different combustion chamber, these technologies offer the hope that zero-carbon flight will be possible. The concepts are still at early stages of development but a green option for aviation is emerging.

Summary

The process of transition will require political, social and technological change. Technological change is within our grasp and we could probably develop a roadmap of the changes required, timescales and dependencies, and allocate responsibilities to a variety of stakeholders. Social and political changes on the other hand, are likely to be far more complex. Different political ideologies would have to be reconciled, any readjustment of power or influence would need to be managed, and building support for a new vision of a society would require consensus across multiple different parts of society. Social and economic transformation is going to require communication and stakeholder engagement on a level that has never been seen before.

12

Action Plans for Governments

Chapter summary

This chapter considers the actions that need to be taken by governments to influence market forces and the areas where policy reform is required. It identifies key areas of policymaking and looks at the need for political accountability and transparency.

Intergovernmental action

Action to reverse climate change will require extraordinary leadership by the major emitters of greenhouse gases, particularly China, India and the US, and all nations will need to find a common purpose rather than pursue individual strategies. Achieving consensus across the international community has been difficult so far and further progress will require the UN to have greater authority. In particular, the 2015 Paris Agreement needs to be overhauled so that targets are mandatory, not voluntary, and the aggregated plans of all nations need to be adjusted so that the remaining carbon budget is not exceeded. The limits on total emissions must be set at a level that is consistent with a maximum rise in global temperatures of 1.5°C. National monitoring and reporting will need to be strengthened. The current situation of voluntary targets, poor monitoring, false reporting and negligible consequences for countries that breach their self-determined targets is woefully inadequate and we are deluding ourselves if we believe such ineffective measures will avert climate catastrophe.

Converting new commitments into hard action will require the authority of the UN to be strengthened and international agreements to be underpinned by a number of core principles. For example:

- All countries share in the cost of the transition.
- No country benefits by remaining outside the agreement.
- Non-compliance to have repercussions on rogue nations.
- Shared response to world events, such as: drought, famine, floods and migration.

Overhaul the Conference of the Parties

The annual meeting of the COP is failing to achieve the levels of commitment that are required. The UN currently appears to lack the capacity to define a global strategy for transformation and the call by Sir David Attenborough for *a plan* appears to be a long way off.

The pace of intergovernmental activity will need to increase dramatically. We have a few years left to achieve the necessary changes, yet the COP meets once a year. There has to be a radical shake-up in the way that this process is managed. The UN is failing to achieve the necessary shift in political thinking. Part of the reason for this may be that it suits some of the more influential nations to curtail the authority of the UN. Therefore, the authority of the UN has to be freed from the influence of individual national interests. In addition, strategy, structure, systems and organizational competencies of the UN have to be overhauled.

Action by national governments

While it needs to be emphasized that the rate of change is too slow, it is important to acknowledge that some countries are making progress: four nations have formally passed laws that commit them to achieving net zero by 2050: UK, France, Denmark and New Zealand. A more ambitious commitment of net zero by 2045 has been set by Sweden and Scotland. A number of other countries have set targets for net zero by 2050, although the commitments have not yet been formalized in law.[1]

The UK commitment to become net zero by 2050 is an important turning point in government policy and although this declaration is relatively recent, it is a much-welcomed shift in policy. It illustrates how quickly things can change in politics. For example, it was only a few years previously, during the 2017 election, that the Conservative Party manifesto identified *Five Giant Challenges*.

1. The need for a strong economy.
2. Brexit and a changing world.
3. Enduring social divisions.
4. An ageing society.
5. Fast changing technology.

At this point, the environment was not listed as one of the major challenges. This omission probably reflects the fact that political parties design election manifestos to appeal to voters and the absence of the environment from this list may be a reflection of the voting public's perceived lack of concern for environmental issues. Whatever the reason, the environment is now high on the government's priorities and there is much to be commended within recent UK environmental policy. Although the UK by itself will only have a minimal impact on slowing global warming, the UK is setting an example of responsible environmental leadership. In addition, it will position the UK economy at the forefront of green innovation, the so-called *first-mover advantage*. As discussed earlier, a policy gap still needs to be bridged, but the positive actions now being taken are important and deserve to be recognized.

Overall, the UK contributes about 1 per cent of global carbon emissions so its immediate impact will be small. Total greenhouse gas emissions by Europe are less than that of North America and only a quarter of the Asia-Pacific region. If the Paris 2015 targets are to be reached, it will be essential that China and the US achieve net zero by 2050. Unfortunately, progress in the US has been slow and the Trump administration showed little enthusiasm for the 2015 Paris Agreement. This was emphasized when President Trump threatened to pull out of the Paris Agreement. China, on the other hand, has announced that it will be net zero before 2060. The benefits to China will be that, not only does it seek to mitigate the damaging consequences of climate change on its own economy, but it will also develop a technical advantage in sustainable technologies, as well as strengthening its reputation in the global community.[2]

The battle between economic growth and the environment is likely to continue. Over the next 50 years, we will see a rapidly growing global population, growth in consumer demand and increased pressure to exploit natural resources. These resources will include the essentials for human survival: fertile agricultural land and water. It is self-evident that the potential for new conflicts will be ever-present. The last 100 years have seen a succession of conflicts, and the underlying reasons invariably link to a desire to secure access to the sources of wealth, such as oil and other natural resources. These conflicts have left a legacy of economic and political turmoil that continue to be reported regularly in the news that flashes across our screens each day: the Middle East, Palestine and South America. The list goes on.

Although self-interest can drive conflict, it can also provide the impetus to heal the wounds of conflict. For example, the cold war between the USSR and the West eventually began to thaw, and relations between the US and China finally evolved from distrust and isolationism to a state of economic interdependence. However, these political achievements look increasingly perilous. Improved relationships were based on a mutual desire for shared wealth through trade; however, this cooperation is increasingly under threat from isolationist and protectionist policies. This risk was highlighted by the trade wars between China and the US, as the Trump administration reacted to a growing trade deficit with China. Effective international cooperation will need to be based on shared economic benefits. However, there is a risk that some corporations and countries might seek to take control of the new sources of energy causing new international tensions and rivalries.

Global interdependency

Although the above paragraphs summarize a hugely complex set of issues in a simplistic way, the basic proposition is that pressure on resources threatens to divide us, but shared opportunities can unite us. Therefore, we need to seek mutually beneficial economic outcomes from the transition to a sustainable society. Unless we use the next few decades as an opportunity to build international alliances, then we face a period of global transition that will create new geo-political conflicts as countries and corporations seek to exploit those parts of the world that provide the resources essential for the post-industrial global economy. Foreign policy strategies may discard the oil-rich areas of the world in favour of alliances (or control) with the nations that have the new high-value resources such as minerals, fresh water and fertile land.

We have arrived at a position were a handful of dominant nations account for the majority of global trade. The US and China account for over 30 per cent of global GDP and commercial power is increasingly concentrated in the hands of a few global corporations. The ultimate endpoint of this trajectory is that a handful of corporations will control not just global resources and commercial activity but also control political strategy at national and international levels.

The distribution of wealth within many countries is creating ever-increasing inequality where the top 1 per cent of the population controls an increasing proportion of the wealth. At the same time, we are seeing the collapse of the middle-class. This once secure social group is increasingly characterized by having little job security, high debt and an uncertain future. Added to this, there is a growing proportion of people in poorly paid, undesirable, temporary work that often fails to provide the basic necessities of life, even by working long hours and multiple jobs.

The mantras that *wealth is good* and that the *trickle-down effect benefits all* have failed to deliver the promised benefits. The social injustice caused by traditional theories on business and the economy is resulting in the emergence of new business philosophies. The phrase *purpose before profit* is beginning to gain acceptance within the corporate world. The concept of a 'B Corp', derived from the phrase *benefit corporation*, is also gaining traction in the business world. These shifts in corporate thinking offer hope that an emerging corporate ethos will pursue objectives beyond growth and profit. A key feature of these emerging business philosophies is sense of accountability for environmental impact. However, while some organizations are adopting new corporate values, others remain entrenched in values that prioritize profit maximization and see an opportunity to exploit their more socially responsible competitors. Therefore, driving changes in corporate values and behaviours will require legislation that sets out social and environmental obligations.

In the UK, there have been a number of new regulations that require corporations to report on the environmental impact of their activities. In April 2019, Parliament introduced the *Streamlined Energy and Carbon Reporting Act* (SECR). This legislation places specific obligations on directors to monitor and report on their environmental impact. While these declarations are important, these reporting requirements are not a replacement for policies that set corporate standards and environmental obligations.

The scale and complexity of the task of achieving changes in corporate behaviour is overwhelming and it is easy to get lost in the detail, so it is worth starting with the two overriding priorities:

- Reduce greenhouse gas emissions to net zero by 2050.
- Protect the natural environment, in particular: stop the destruction of rain forests, recover lost forests, protect the fertility of the land, and reverse desertification.

All governments need to address these two priorities. Failure to do so will make any other goals irrelevant. For example, policies to adopt the principles of a circular economy and reduce plastic pollution, while important, are irrelevant if levels of global warming take us past the tipping point. Yes, we need to do all the other good stuff, but we must not lose sight of the primary threat and the timescale that we are on.

Characteristics of effective policies

One of the characteristics of effective policies is that they should address the *causes* rather than simply alleviating the symptoms. For example, it is futile to take actions that reduce symptoms, such as building flood defences, while continuing to produce greenhouse gases that warm the planet. Ever-higher walls will not solve the problem. Effective policies should have clearly defined objectives and there should be clearly defined criteria for assessing their effectiveness. For example:

Policies to influence consumer behaviour

- Information: Consumers and corporations need to understand how their activities affect global warming, pollution and the destruction of the natural environment.
- Incentives: Taxes, grants and subsidies designed to steer consumer behaviour and corporate activity away from activities that are environmentally damaging.
- Cost effective: Any market intervention through government policies will influence how resources are allocated between alternative uses. This requires an understanding of opportunity cost, as well as cost/benefit analysis.
- Future certainty: All policies will need to provide consumers and organizations with a reasonable degree of certainty about the future so that they can plan for the medium to longer term.

Policies to reduce CO_2 emissions

- Cost effectiveness assessed in terms of reduction in emissions of CO_2 tonnes equivalent (CO_2Te) per million pounds.
- Speed of implementation identifies how quickly CO_2Te reductions can be achieved. For example, it would be more important to achieve reduction in CO_2Te within five years, rather than wait for a more cost-effective technology to be available in 15 or 20 years.
- Scale of impact: Some policies might be cost-effective but only deliver a small reduction in carbon emissions.

- Social benefit reflects how the policy might deliver wider social objectives. For example, thermal insulation of low-income housing will help reduce energy demand and support social objectives.

Policies to influence corporate activity

Policies to influence corporate activity will need to make organizations accountable for the environmental costs of their activities. Examples might include:

- A corporate law requiring organizations to declare damage to the environment against auditable criteria that link to the principle of *polluter pays*.
- A polluter pays tax system that reflects the full environmental cost.
- Transparency of vested interests to show which organizations and individuals benefit from corporate actions that damage the environment (as revealed by the auditable criteria/ polluter pays).

Other characteristics of effective policies will include:

Consistent with the social contract

Effective policies should be consistent with the implicit social contract, as espoused by Rousseau's 1762 treatise on the concept of the social contract, between a government and those it represents. The principle of the social contract is based on the idea that individuals surrender some of their freedoms in exchange for the greater good. Perhaps there is a need for an *environmental social contract* that requires citizens to accept that government intervention is required to transform the global economic and social model, without which our current civilization will not survive.

Corporate-consumer focus

Policies on the environment should focus on the interdependency between corporations and consumers.

- Corporate responsibility: Requirements that organizations audit their activities and report on their performance, including providing information to the consumers that use their products and services. This will require mechanisms to assess the environmental impact of organizations, plus the ability to hold organizations to account when they breach relevant regulations or legislation.
- Consumer awareness and concern: Consumers need appropriate information so that they understand how the products and services that they buy affect the environment, enabling them to make informed purchase decisions. Informed consumer decisions will drive environmentally responsible corporate strategies.

Measurable outcomes

Effective policies should deliver the intended outcomes. In the case of policies designed to achieve net zero by 2050, policies should be aligned with clear goals and targets. For example:

- Goal: Reduce CO_2 emission – national total:
  - 50 per cent reduction by 2030.
  - 80 per cent reduction by 2040.
  - Net zero by 2050.
- Targets: Reduce emission targets for vehicles:
  - 15 per cent reduction by 2025.
  - 45 per cent reduction by 2030.
  - 75 per cent reduction by 2040.
  - Net zero by 2050.

Financial resources

The process of economic transition will require massive investment in energy, transport, housing, industry and agriculture. The cost will have to be managed by government with levels of borrowing not seen since times of war. Political parties need to demonstrate their commitment to invest in a green future and establish green banks to channel finance into long-term investment.

Key policy areas

Having identified some of the characteristics of effective policy we can now look at some of the key policy areas that governments need to address.

Energy: production and distribution

As already discussed, the rapid transition to a net zero carbon society will not be achieved through free-market forces, and political parties will need to intervene in the energy market and create the structures, standards, regulations and controls that will provide the certainty necessary for long-term planning and investment. Political parties will need to demonstrate that they have clear policies to address the following:

- Nuclear energy: The economic viability of nuclear energy will collapse if the real economic cost of nuclear, across the full lifecycle, including storage/disposal of waste and decommissioning, is born by the consumer. Full cost pricing and transparency of the economic models used to evaluate nuclear is essential when justifying its role in the short to medium term.
- Renewables: Renewables are increasingly important but achieving a rapid transition to renewables will require incentives and certainty in energy policy. Political parties must have a clear energy strategy with supporting evidence of how this will be achieved within the fastest possible timescale.
- Load balancing: Any energy strategy will need to integrate appropriate technologies to provide effective load balancing. This will require policies that create the market mechanisms to encourage solutions such as battery storage, including connecting EVs into smart grids, and other energy storage systems such as hydrogen/ammonia and kinetic energy solutions.
- Intelligent grids: Huge investment will be required to enable cities and regions to establish smart grids and this will be accompanied by a shift to localized energy generation and less reliance on a national grid. In addition, the capacity of the

grid systems will need to be increased as energy loads could rise by a factor of three to five. Regulating the load to ensure that parts of the system do not overload will be as important as balancing peaks and troughs in the energy supply.

Energy efficiency

Policies to reduce domestic and industrial energy usage need to be clearly defined. Particular areas of focus will include the capture of waste industrial heat, solar water heaters, LED lighting and building insulation. Such policies need long-term commitment rather than the uncertainty over recent years when regulations have been introduced and then changed after a few years.

Agriculture

Agricultural practices have an enormous impact on the environment. In the advanced economies, we see intensive farming methods, especially animal agriculture and intensive crop rotations. These practices are degrading the land and damaging the environment. In emerging economies, we see subsistence farmers and indigenous people whose land is degraded due to overworking, soil erosion and poor farming practices.

Farmers already understand the need to protect the land and reduce their environmental impact, but many farmers will not have the financial reserves to enable them to invest in equipment and technologies that support sustainable farming. Government policy should provide loans and grants to ensure that sustainable farming practices are economically viable. It should also introduce guidelines and regulations to encourage the adoption of best practice and reduce the most damaging impacts of poor farming practice. Examples of government intervention will include:

- Grants and loans: Financial support to meet the cost of investment in sustainable farming practices, for example:
  - Equipment to capture waste from intensive animal farming, including methods to prevent run-off and protect rivers and ground water.

- Equipment to capture methane from waste and convert into energy.
- Adoption of innovative farming methods to reduce chemical fertilizers and insecticides, including linking agricultural equipment to land mapping systems.
- Education and training: Government investment in advice, education and training will enable farming communities to share best practice and adopt new approaches to farming sustainably. Examples include:
  - Encouraging alternative farming practices.
  - Conservation in farming.
  - Nutrient management.
  - Regulation of insecticides and chemicals.
  - Reforesting the countryside.
  - Greater value being attributed to set aside land.
- Regulation: The shift to more sustainable farming will require stronger regulation and standards.
  - Strict control and, where necessary, banning of agricultural chemicals, with particular focus on pesticides that are linked to the decline of insect life.
  - Guidelines and regulations to control any changes to land use that might cause damage to areas that sustain wildlife and support biodiversity.
  - Regulations on emissions and animal waste/effluent to reduce pollutants and damage to the environment.
- Traceability in the agricultural supply chain: Farming has a complex supply chain. For example, the demand for animal feedstock is a primary factor in the destruction of the Amazon. Forest is being converted into farmland for producing crops used in animal feedstock. The advanced economies need to ensure traceability of the agricultural supply chain.
  - Restrictions on products that come from compromised sources.
  - Manufacturers required to audit suppliers.
  - International agreements to ban the import of products from specified sources.

The urgent need to make farming more sustainable was highlighted in 2017 by, Michael Gove, Secretary of State for the Environment:

The UK is 30 to 40 years away from 'the fundamental eradication of soil fertility' in parts of the country, the environment secretary, Michael Gove, has warned.

'We have encouraged a type of farming which has damaged the earth,' Gove told the parliamentary launch of the Sustainable Soils Alliance, (SSA). 'Countries can withstand coups d'état, wars and conflict, even leaving the EU, but no country can withstand the loss of its soil and fertility.'

'If you have heavy machines churning the soil and impacting it, if you drench it in chemicals that improve yields but in the long term undercut the future fertility of that soil, you can increase yields year on year but ultimately you really are cutting the ground away from beneath your own feet. Farmers know that.'[3]

Unless governments take action to encourage alternative farming methods, the soil structure, microorganisms and nutrients will become seriously degraded, causing the quality and output of agriculture to decline dramatically within 30 or 40 years.

Transport

Transport accounts for approximately 25 per cent of CO_2 emissions. Of this, approximately 85 per cent is caused by road transport. As a separate issue, air travel and shipping both cause specific problems; aviation emissions enter higher levels of the atmosphere and shipping emissions are particularly damaging with pollutants caused by the use of low-grade fuels.

EVs offer an immediate solution to conventional vehicles and will bring other benefits associated with load balancing in the energy grid system. The transition to EVs is already happening, but policies are needed to encourage this switch to low emission vehicles and also to secure the intelligent infrastructure necessary to integrate EV battery capacity into the energy grid.

It should not be assumed that we could easily switch to EV. One potential limitation is that current battery technologies are dependent on lithium, nickel and cobalt, and demand on these resources is going to increase exponentially. In addition, the mining and production of these chemicals causes environmental damage and should not be regarded as a sustainable solution to the energy transition. An article on the website www.wired.co.uk offers a useful summary of the environmental issues associated with the growing demand for batteries. It includes the following quote:

> 'Like any mining process, it is invasive, it scars the landscape, it destroys the water table and it pollutes the earth and the local wells,' said Guillermo Gonzalez, a lithium battery expert from the University of Chile, in a 2009 interview. 'This isn't a green solution – it's not a solution at all.'[4]

Alternative battery technologies may become available and hydrogen fuel cells offer an alternative to the ubiquitous adoption of batteries, however, these technologies will need to be developed and commercialized rapidly.

The alternatives for shipping and air travel are less clear and although alternative technologies exist, the challenge of making such technologies commercially viable is likely to be a major obstacle. In the short term it is likely that we will need to reduce the demand for air travel and cleaner fuels will need to be introduced to shipping.

Sustainable cities

The percentage of the global population living in cities is already greater than 50 per cent. In Africa, it is 40 per cent, in Asia it is about 50 per cent, in Europe, it is over 70 per cent and in North America, it is over 80 per cent. This trend to urbanization is projected to increase, creating greater challenges related to waste, energy demand, water use and travel. Future policies will need to encourage the adoption of technologies that enable cities to function effectively, use energy intelligently and provide a safe living environment. This will require new urban infrastructure for intelligent energy grids, energy efficient buildings and green transport systems, including cycle networks and walker-friendly cities. City planning will also need to protect the urban environment by using regulations to protect air quality and deploying technologies that support the circular economy and waste recycling.

Rivers and oceans

Pollution of rivers and oceans is caused by multiple factors, most notably manufacturing, agricultural effluent and abandoned waste. Damage is also caused by industrial-scale fishing, dredging the seabed and other activities that result in rivers and oceans becoming dead zones. Approximately one billion people are dependent on fish as their main source of protein. The industry is worth over $400 billion, yet consistent over-fishing is resulting in declining yields, with one third of fish stocks close to the point of extinction. Action needs to be taken to ensure that fishing is sustainable and to enable fish stocks to recover. Current activities are creating a humanitarian disaster and destroying the livelihoods of hundreds of millions of people.

Waste

Globally, we produce over three million tonnes of waste per day. Per day! In the next 75 years, this is projected to rise to 12 million tonnes of waste per day. Given that it can take 700 years for a plastic bottle to break down, the impact of waste on our planet is a truly horrendous problem. Modern society is unlikely to eliminate the use of plastics, and action to reduce the damage caused by waste will need to focus on recycling, the reduction of one-use plastics and the development of biodegradable plastics.

Refrigerants

Ozone damaging CFCs have now been phased out, but the replacement refrigerants, such as HFC, are significant contributors to climate change. The production, servicing and decommissioning of domestic appliances and air conditioning units has to be effectively regulated and controlled. Regulations to ensure that refrigerants do not escape into the atmosphere, especially at disposal, are imperative. In addition, there will need to be safeguards to ensure that items are not exported to countries where such regulations can be circumvented.

The circular economy

The circular economy encourages the reuse of materials, as opposed to the *linear economy* that extracts raw materials, converts them into economic value and then disposes of products at end of life. If we are to move towards a sustainable economy, the principles of the circular economy will have to be embedded in how goods are produced and consumed.

However, the principle of a circular economy requires some value being attributed to the product at the end of its life. If the value is low, then it will be necessary to impose some form of subsidy or penalty in order to make the process of recycling economically viable. In practice, much of the material that households send for recycling has very little value. In addition, certain types of product, including some plastics, are not practical to recycle. We therefore have a situation where the act of placing items into a recycling bin gives the impression of environmental responsibility, but in practice, much of the product that is sent for recycling is not recovered into a reusable form.

Another limitation of the circular economy is that recycling suffers the effect of entropy, where every transformation of a physical state results in degraded quality. Therefore, a product that reaches the end of its economic life cannot be continually recycled to create a new product. Some value may be recovered but additional energy and resources will be required in the process of recovering useable materials, and the process eventually becomes uneconomic. While recognizing that the circular economy faces some inherent difficulties, there is no doubt that economies will need to embed its principles. We are currently a long way away from a truly circular economy and governments need to address the following problems:

- A low proportion of products are recycled.
- Much of the waste collected for recycling is shipped to less developed parts of the world so that it is out of sight, effectively dumped.
- Waste that is shipped to less developed countries can cause serious environmental damage including pollution of land and water.
- Less developed countries are ill equipped to reprocess waste safely and frequently use dangerous methods. For example, burning items that contain recoverable metals but, in the process, releasing dioxins and other harmful chemicals.

Enabling the shift towards a circular economy is important and some of the practical steps that can be taken include:

- Governments to introduce relevant legislation, taxes, guidelines and regulations.
- Corporates to understand implications of a circular economy for their business model.
- Technology and systems to enable a circular economy to operate effectively, for example block chain.
- Communities and consumers to be actively incentivized to adopt behaviours that enable a circular economy.

Moving towards a more circular economy will help to slow down the rate at which raw materials are extracted from the environment and, if managed effectively, will help to reduce the effects of pollution. However, recycling will only lessen the environmental impact of industrial production rather than eliminate it.

Delivering against policy commitments

The ability to devise appropriate policies that provide the framework for economic transition is only the first part of the story. The next step will be to ensure that such policies are implemented. The following points illustrate some of the factors that will need to be addressed.

Accountability

The concept of the *senior responsible officer* (SRO) needs to be embedded within all organizations. At a political level, this would require presidents, prime ministers and senior ministers to be held responsible for environmental impact. Without clear accountability at the highest level it will be impossible achieve change. Within governments, different ministers should have clear targets that they are accountable for. For example:

- Transport: Targets for transition to zero emission vehicles.
- Buildings: Targets for energy efficient buildings.
- Industry: Targets for resources from sustainable sources.
- Farming: Targets for sustainable farming practices.
- Education: Education syllabus that includes the environment.

Visibility

Government will need to establish methods for collecting reliable data and reporting on progress against targets. Ideally, there should be international standards defined so that data can be collated internationally using consistent methods.

Transition competencies

As identified earlier, during periods of complexity and uncertainty, those that are tasked with leading a period of change will require a specific set of competencies associated with *process* expertise. The competencies will be required at all levels of the public sector:

- Government ministers.
- Civil service.
- Regional government.
- City and town councils.

The competencies will include underpinning skills such as facilitation, stakeholder engagement and the ability to communicate across disparate networks. These can be broadly described as the ability to manage the process of complex change. For example, how to engage the relevant people, in the right way, so that options are identified, prioritized and selected. The other area of expertise is *task* expertise, the technical skills and knowledge required to implement the required changes. This is particularly relevant to the *delivery* capability.

National political consensus

Managing the transition to a sustainable society is going to be a major challenge for governments around the world. Not only do they need to define their strategic response to climate change and build the capability to implement the strategy, but they also need to achieve political consensus to support the radical policies that will be required. This degree of consensus is rarely achieved other than in times of extreme threat, such as war. For many countries, just managing the internal power struggles associated with policymaking will require changes to the dynamics of national politics. The nature of the challenge can be illustrated with reference to the US, where members of the Trump administration were sceptical of the causes of climate change and Congress was unable to achieve consensus on targets for greenhouse gas reduction. This type of problem is not limited to the US and many countries struggle to achieve political consensus on issues relating to climate change.

International collaboration

Governments around the world will need to achieve consensus on both the scale of response that is required and the times scales. This response has been described as a *war footing* in that the nations of the world need to mobilize their economic resources in ways that are normally only seen in times of war.

- National governments need to acknowledge the climate emergency and move to a *war footing*.
- The need to refocus on national economic efforts to meet the challenge of a global transition.

The role of intergovernmental organizations

Intergovernmental organizations will have an increasingly important role to play and the following list of actions illustrates the types of activity that we would expect to see from organizations such as the UN, World Bank and IMF. While these organizations *may* have strategies to guide the transition to a zero-carbon future, they do not seem to have been shared widely. The types of areas that would need to be addressed are illustrated below.

Transition strategy

A united response by all governments is essential. This will require:

- A clear mandate for intergovernmental organizations to lead and manage a transition process.
- A commitment from national governments that they endorse the authority of the appointed intergovernmental authority.
- Mechanisms and authority to secure compliance, by all nations, to the transition strategy.
- Appropriate systems and processes to ensure effective governance.

Intergovernmental structures and systems

It will be essential to strengthen the monitoring and reporting authority of the UN. Particular areas of focus will include:

- Set clear targets for the reduction of greenhouse gases for each national economy.
- Set targets that are consistent with achieving a 1.5°C limit to global warming.
- Monitor each national government performance against the key drivers of global warming (GHG emissions and destruction of rain forests).
- Power to impose sanctions/penalties on countries that breach their national targets.
- Implement and manage the enabling structures and systems.

For example:
- Introduce and manage an international carbon trading mechanism.
- Set international regulations to control the use of products and resources, such as the use of palm oil.
- Enforceable standards in areas such as agriculture and the production/disposal of chemicals, particularly refrigerants.

Funding for global transition

The role of the IMF should be enhanced to support a global economic transition with particular focus on:

- Managing the decline of industries linked to the carbon economy.
- Providing investment for the transition to sustainable industries.
- Providing funding to compensate nations and industry sectors adversely affected by the transition.

There is no natural law that states that human civilization will survive, indeed, all the evidence shows that civilizations rise and fall, with many of them disappearing forever. The potential scenarios facing our current civilization suggest that we might be able to delay the impact of climate change, but unless we address fundamental aspects of how our society operates then our civilization will not survive.

13

Personal Accountability

Chapter summary

This chapter considers the actions that individuals will need to take in order to achieve the transition to a more sustainable society. This behavioural change will require policies and legislation that encourage patterns of consumption and behaviours consistent with living sustainably. Government intervention may be able to influence social behaviour, but ultimately, individuals will need to understand the reasons for change and the consequences if we continue on the current trajectory.

Introduction

Living in a sustainable world will require changes in the way that we live our lives. It is important that these changes bring consumer benefits rather than be regarded as a sacrifice *for the greater good*. Achieving changes in consumer behaviour will require policies that provide a combination of incentives, such as grants, plus disincentives such as taxes. In addition, the new generation of goods and services must be desirable to consumers by offering benefits that encourage changes in consumer behaviour. For example, the switch to EVs will offer consumer benefits, such as lower running costs. They will also bring other benefits, particularly in towns and cities where vehicle noise and air pollution will be greatly reduced. Similarly, energy efficient buildings will lower household bills and create a more comfortable living environment. Consumers should have expectations of living in energy efficient housing in the same way that we currently wish to live in houses that have double glazing and central heating.

The other important area where change needs to occur is agricultural practices. Current farming practices are unsustainable. In the developed world, the quality of land is being degraded by intensive farming practices. In the emerging world, pressure on resources, poor farming methods and lack of water is leading to desertification. This has to change. Adopting sustainable farming practices is perfectly feasible and there are many examples where farmers are already taking action to reverse the damage caused by intensive farming. Changing agricultural practices may, in the short term, result in lower yields and it is important to acknowledge that lower yields will result in higher food prices, particularly those items that had previously depended on intensive farming practices. As a result, farming practices are likely to focus on the food staples that are naturally suited to their own geographic region. Sustainable living will mean changes to our diets, but it does not mean that people will go hungry. It does not even have to result in an increase in the typical household food bill, but it will probably mean that the types of food many people buy will change. Failure to adopt sustainable farming methods might allow cheap food to remain in the shops over the short term, but within a couple of decades agricultural yields will irretrievably collapse in an age where global population is predicted by the UN to be approximately 10 billion by 2050.

In addition to the need to adopt sustainable farming techniques, it is essential that we stop destroying rain forests and other natural environments in order to create agricultural land for beef ranching and the production of animal feedstock. A report by the UN Food and Agricultural Organization (FAO) outlines some of the impacts of livestock farming on the environment. The following three sections identify some of the key figures and statistics.

> Twenty-six percent of the Planet's ice-free land is used for livestock grazing and 33 percent of croplands are used for livestock feed production. Livestock contribute to seven percent of the total greenhouse gas emissions through enteric fermentation and manure.

The livestock sector is one of the key drivers of land-use change. Each year, 13 billion hectares of forest area are lost due to land conversion for agricultural uses as pastures or cropland, for both food and livestock feed crop production. This has detrimental effects on regional water availability, soil fertility, biodiversity and climate change. Furthermore, 20 percent of the world grasslands are degraded; this trend is increasing, mainly due to intensified animal density per area.

As livestock density increases and is in closer confines with wildlife and humans, there is a growing risk of disease that threatens every single one of us: 66 percent of the emerging diseases in humans have animal origins and one or two new diseases emerge every year.[1]

Many people will still want to eat meat and dairy products but adopting a philosophy of *less but better* will have a direct impact on the environment. Consumers will need to become more concerned about where and how their food was produced. This change in consumer behaviour is premised on an understanding of the environmental cost of meat and dairy production, coupled with knowledge about the health benefits of a low meat diet.

Personal responsibilities

Responsibility for living sustainably cannot be abdicated to politicians. Ultimately, individuals are responsible for the choices they make and the impact that they have on the environment. The following points offer a brief summary of actions that individuals can take.

Stay well informed

Each of us has a responsibility to educate ourselves so that we understand the environmental threats that face the planet, the causes and the actions that are required. We need to understand the environmental impact of our purchase decisions, to understand how our actions create a carbon footprint and to determine what changes we need to make in our daily lives.

Responsible consumption

The age of the throwaway society is over and the age of responsible consumption is upon us. As responsible consumers, we should evaluate our requirements against the environmental impact of consuming the various products or services. If we have little need for an item but there is a high environmental impact, then we should either not buy it or find an equivalent that will have little environmental impact. Such changes in consumer behaviour require relevant information to be available to the consumer in much the same way that food packaging provides information on calories, sugars and fats. If we understand the environmental cost, we can make informed decisions. There may be fears that this might result in lower consumption, lower economic growth and poorer living standards as sales of environmentally damaging products and services decline. In practice, organizations would divert their effort to finding new, more sustainable products and services to offer. It is a fallacy to believe that a sustainable society could not be a wealthy society.

Reuse and recycling

Societies have to stop throwing stuff into landfill. As individuals, we have to take personal responsibility for disposing of unwanted items. Items should be recycled or reused wherever possible and we should make purchase decisions that take account of the ability to recycle items at end of life. However, the ability of individuals to take responsibility for recycling is often dependent on the provision of services to collect and recycle household waste. For example, an individual may be concerned that throwing an empty printer cartridge into the bin is wrong, yet there may be no easy way to ensure that it will be recycled. The process of returning used items for recycling has to be as easy as the process of buying the product in the first place. Ideally, the market will create innovative mechanisms to encourage people to return used items to the point of purchase, but this will require the used items to have some value. It is likely that regulation will be required in order to stimulate a market for collecting and recycling product.

Consumer pressure on organizations

Consumer pressure will be an important factor in encouraging organizations to be environmentally responsible, but ultimately this needs to be underpinned by legislation. If we change our patterns of consumption, we will force corporations to change their products and service. This pressure on producers can gain momentum by influencing others, and individuals can help shift opinions by talking about the changes they are making and the reasons why it is important. Another way to put pressure on organizations is to support petitions and campaigns to highlight damaging activity by organizations. This activity is influencing the decisions being made in boardrooms and by policy makers, but, ultimately, this type of pressure must come from informed purchase decisions by individuals. Individuals cannot be continually extolled to campaign against specific causes, as *petition fatigue* will quickly set in.

Influence employers

Employees have an important role in encouraging organizations to operate sustainably; if employees care about the environment then organizations care. Even if most employees do not influence corporate strategy, many employees will have the opportunity to raise concerns and propose changes. There is also a growing tendency among job seekers to find roles that provide a sense of purpose that goes beyond profit maximization. Organizations that want to attract applicants will increasingly need to demonstrate social and environmental credibility.

Collaboration

Individuals are most effective when they collaborate to achieve a shared purpose. As individuals, we should seek ways to collaborate with other groups or organizations that are addressing the issues we care about. An example of environmental collaboration is a group in the bay area of San Francisco called *Bay Area Climate Action* (BACA). This was started by a small group of individuals who organized a couple of events to discuss the implications of climate change in the Bay Area. The Bay Area has approximately 100 towns and cities and a population close to seven million. The group brought together government and civic representatives, academics, climate activists, religious groups and other stakeholders from the community. This initiative has enabled public sector bodies to work with other stakeholders to develop strategies and ensure that the Bay Area is better prepared for the consequences of climate change.

Environmental activism

Ultimately, social and economic change needs to occur at a political level, but politicians are invariably reluctant to disrupt the status quo. Therefore, it seems inevitable that some level of environmental activism will be required before politicians take action. Activism can take many forms and sometimes this includes disruptive methods to draw media attention. As public fears and concerns grow, it is likely that activist groups will gain more support. Hopefully, political parties will recognize growing public concerns and use this as an opportunity to develop sustainable policies that will build their political support before activism becomes too disruptive. However, if the political establishment fail to respond to growing concerns then disruptive activities are likely to occur.

Political engagement

Most political parties have affiliated groups that are concerned about environmental issues. Involvement with these groups may provide an opportunity to contribute ideas and influence policy but it can also be a frustrating process as political parties can be poor at connecting with individual party members. Perseverance is essential, coupled with the ability to identify influential allies.

Checklist for individuals

Here is a summary of practical actions:

- Dramatically reduce consumption of beef, dairy products and other products associated with animal agriculture.
- Reduce domestic energy consumption, for example, invest in efficient domestic heating, home insulation and only heat rooms being used.
- Avoid unnecessary car journeys, use public transport where practical and switch to low, ideally, zero-emission vehicles.
- Avoid or minimize air travel, in particular, plan holidays that avoid long-distance air travel.
- Use energy suppliers that source 100 per cent of power from renewable energies.
- Minimize impulse consumption; don't buy things for the sake of it.
- Identify and buy from those organizations that are leading their industry sector in environmental responsibility.
- Support local activities that are integral to sustainable communities, such as farmer markets.
- Be aware of the environmental impact of different purchase decisions, for example:
  - Take account of the environmental impact of the textile industry; for example, the manufacture of one T-shirt will require over 3,000 litres of water due to irrigation of cotton fields and manufacturing/dying processes.
  - Seek out foods that are sustainably sourced.
  - Avoid products with palm oil, frequently found in cooking oil, processed foods and cosmetics.
  - Avoid *throwaway* plastic items.
  - Verify the energy efficiency rating of electrical products before purchase.
- Review financial investments and pension schemes; seek out portfolios that offer ethical packages and invest in *positive impact* funds.
- Vote for the political party that is most genuinely concerned and competent to address the causes of climate change.

- Get involved with one of the major political parties so that your views and opinions can be expressed.
- Get involved with local organizations that influence your region and communities, including parish councils, civic societies, local councils, charitable bodies.

Four key interdependencies

There is a complex interdependency between individuals, corporations, society and the political process. Achieving change in one area may be dependent upon changes in another area. Therefore, we cannot treat each of these areas in isolation; instead, we need to address change within all four areas.

Figure 13.1: Four key interdependencies

Political

Individuals understand and support legislation

Corporations recognize that legislation supports long term objectives

Individual ← → Corporate

Individuals acknowledge personal responsibility & society judges individuals

Corporate activity accountable to society & society judges organizations

Society

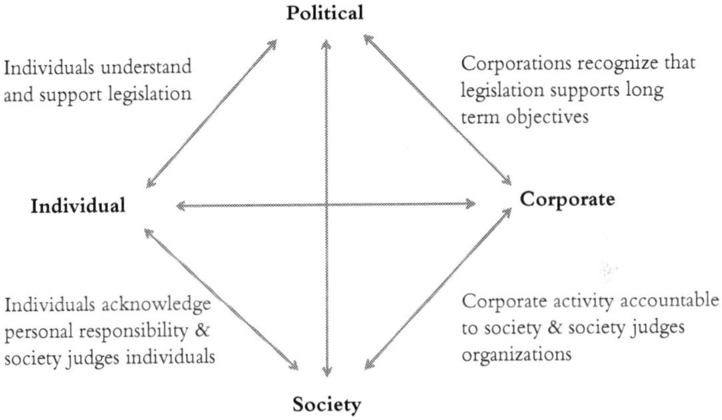

Source: Richard Joy

Those wishing to effect change need to recognize that influence and pressure has to be coordinated across all four areas. For example, Figure 13.1 above illustrates how each area will influence a switch to biodegradable packaging:

- Corporate: Responding to consumer demand and compliance with policies to encourage the use of biodegradable materials.

- Individual: Greater awareness of the need to reduce plastic pollution.
- Society: A shift in social norms so that one-use plastic packaging is regarded as unacceptable.
- Political: Policies that respond to public pressure for legislation on one-use plastic packaging.

Individual self-reflection

Finally, it might be useful for each of us to look deeper into our own motivations and behaviours. Unless we understand our own behaviours, it is presumptive to assume what factors might influence the behaviour of others. The sorts of questions we need to ask ourselves might include:

- Whom do I blame: corporates, vested interests, politicians, *them*, myself?
- What is the environmental impact of my current lifestyle; what is my carbon footprint?
- What aspects of my life cause the most damage to the environment?
- What lifestyle changes do I need to make to reduce my environmental impact?
- Why do I fail to take effective action?
- What would motivate me to take action?
- How can I raise awareness of the issues that concern me?

This chapter has examined some of the actions we as individuals can take in order to support the transition to a sustainable society. We cannot absolve ourselves from the responsibility of taking action to reduce our impact on the environment. Although our individual efforts might be minor, collectively our impact will be significant. We are the change.

14

A New Political Movement

Chapter summary

This chapter considers whether the established political parties have the appropriate ideological perspective to drive the transition to a sustainable society. Ultimately, it may require a new political movement to disrupt the alliances between political parties and vested interests. If the current political system fails to reverse global warming, then the stability of our democratic systems is likely to be disrupted by the economic upheavals that will result from climate change. Extremist parties will be able to exploit unemployment, hardship and a growing social divide. International collaboration may be replaced by isolationist policies and nationalistic sentiments. Simplistic solutions by authoritarian leaders will gain popularity as the failings of the traditional political parties are exposed.

Introduction

The last few years have seen a number of national governments implement environmentally responsible policies. In particular, many European countries are investing heavily in renewable energy and there are policies to phase out the production of petrol/diesel vehicles. There have been many positive changes, and these should be acknowledged, but in spite of this, the pace of change is not sufficient. Carbon emissions continue to rise and it seems unlikely that global temperatures will be kept below 1.5°C. Latest projections indicate that the carbon budget associated with the 1.5°C threshold will be breached by 2028.

The current political system is failing to deliver the scale of change required and it seems that the pace of change is determined by economic considerations rather than environmental considerations. This is evidenced within both national and international political processes where the prevailing ideology is that *growth is good*. While this remains the political priority, the primary driver of climate change will not be addressed.

The following quotation from the Pope's 2015 encyclical offers a powerful summary:[1]

> The alliance between the economy and technology ends up side-lining anything unrelated to its immediate interests. Consequently, the most one can expect is superficial rhetoric, sporadic acts of philanthropy and perfunctory expressions of concern for the environment, whereas any genuine attempt by groups within society to introduce change is viewed as a nuisance based on romantic illusions or an obstacle to be circumvented.

Challenging the status quo

There is an overwhelming imperative to transition to an environmentally sustainable society, yet the current political structures are more focused on serving the interests of the major corporates, the banks and the select group of people that control much of the world's wealth. For the last 70 years, our political structures have enabled advanced economies to generate economic growth, improve living standards and insulate themselves from the worst consequences of an unstable world. Consequently, most of us acceded to a political system that largely served our own interests.

This is now changing; the global economy and emerging technologies are driving us towards an economic world with declining job security, ever-widening wealth inequality and the increasingly rapid destruction of the environment. We are on a trajectory that is destabilizing society and destroying the planet. Until recently, most of us in the countries with advanced economies had accepted that some parts of the world suffered injustice, poverty and an incessant series of minor wars, persuading ourselves that such events were outside of our control or influence. We were aware that rain forests were being destroyed, oceans polluted and wildlife threatened. We recognized that there was much that was wrong in the world, but we felt helpless to affect change. There was probably also a sense that events in distant lands did not affect us directly. Our acquiescence to a flawed economic system was due to the fact that it was better to accept an imperfect system rather than embark on a painful and costly journey to achieve change, especially when the system largely served our own interests. This is no longer true; the current political system serves the interests of an ever-smaller group of people and most of us face a dangerous and uncertain future.

Challenging the political status quo

One of the challenges for the environmental movement is to drive the change to a sustainable society at a rate that is fast enough to prevent global warming passing the tipping point yet at a pace of change that is acceptable. The critical element here is the definition of *acceptable*. Acceptable to whom and what factors influence their assessment of acceptability. Ultimately, this revolves around who benefits and who pays the cost.

If political parties are to implement effective environmental policies they will need to demonstrate to their supporters that change brings benefits, but this will only happen when their supporters understand that the potential benefits outweigh the costs. Until then, they will prefer the status quo.

Political parties will only make the environment high on their political agenda if the required policies do not adversely affect their main supporters. In many democracies, this means that any policies to address climate change have to be introduced at a pace that will not significantly damage the profitability of business, particularly those organizations that influence the political fortunes of the political parties.

This is not to say that governments have never introduced policies that business resisted, but the political implications are always weighed carefully. Indeed, there have been some surprisingly bold policy initiatives in the last few years, such as the UK's proposals to ban sales of petrol and diesel vehicles by 2035. However, to be successful, such innovative environmental policies require a *sweet spot* where the public understand the need for a new policy, where the policy brings economic and social benefits and where the industry sectors affected can see potential benefits. With regard to the government's decision to ban petrol and diesel vehicles, there is a sweet spot where the public accept the need to adopt low- or zero-emission vehicles, the government see an opportunity to boost industry and employment through green growth, and the manufactures see an opportunity for their businesses, potentially supported by government intervention such as tax and grant incentives on zero-emission vehicles and the charging infrastructure.[2]

Principles for a new political movement

Until recently, the environmental movement has been represented by minority interest groups or political parties with relatively little influence. Radical environmental thinking is needed, either from the mainstream political parties or from a strong, environmental movement. Any new political movement would not necessarily require a new political party but might seek change through influence on the existing parties.

Ideally, such an influence should operate at both national and international levels to create a political movement that offers a cohesive strategy at a global level. It is difficult to prescribe the structure and modus operandi of any such new political movement, but it might be that it would *work in parallel* with the current political parties. The objective would be to promote a vision for an alternative society, to inspire public support and to build the competencies necessary to manage such a transition.

Environmental movements are gaining support, but it is not clear to what extent they might directly engage with the political establishment. At the moment, most environmental activity is attacking from the outside. This is helping to drive change, but it needs to become integrated with the established political process.

Bodies such as Extinction Rebellion have provided a rallying cry for those concerned about the environment, yet, in spite of the publicity and impact created by its activities, Extinction Rebellion (XR) has not yet engaged effectively with mainstream voters. Many in the environmental movement might agree with their sentiments, but XR has failed to unify the environmental movement. The existing political parties have been quick to distant themselves from XR, and many politicians have condemned them for the disruptive tactics employed.

Greta Thunberg has probably done more than anyone else in the last few years to raise awareness of the imminent threat to the planet. Inevitably, she has been attacked by those that see her ideas as a threat, but in spite of this, she has continued to challenge world leaders and has raged against the inaction by both politicians and the corporate world. To their credit, some individual political leaders, and the UN in particular, have provided her with a platform to hold leaders to account and demand action. However, it is difficult to align Greta Thunberg with a specific political movement. The movement, Schools Strikes for Climate, has grown out of her ideas, but this is a protest group not a coordinated political movement. It still feels as though we are lacking a unifying political movement that can attract mainstream support for a transition to a sustainable society.

It will be difficult to secure support for a new political direction if the electorate believes that the current system serves their needs. Political parties invariably present an overly optimistic view of the future, and until the electorate understand the threats that are about to overwhelm them, then pressure for change will be muted.

Changing the relationship between finance and politics

There has been a growing sense within many Western democracies that the economic system is designed to protect a minority of organizations and their financial interests but fails to serve the needs of significant proportions of the population. The financial crash of 2007–2009 is one example of how powerful individuals and institutions engineered a financial system to generate great wealth for themselves, yet they were granted immunity from the consequences of their actions when the global economy collapsed. 'The crisis stripped workers of livelihoods, decent wages, security and often a roof over their heads. But it did not threaten financialised capitalism. On the contrary: the crisis solidified the existing globalised financial order.'[3]

This quote from Ann Pettifor (*The Case for the Green New Deal*, 2020) is presented in the context of her wider argument that the monetary system has been hijacked by financial institutions for their own purposes rather than serving the needs of society. She goes on to say: 'The big question is this: how to transform Financialised capitalism? How to wrestle power over the great public good that is the monetary system away from the few that exercise private authority over the system? How to restore this great good to public democratic authority?'

In July 2008, an article was published in *New Economics Foundation* that described the *triple crunch*: the credit crisis, climate change and high oil prices:

> These three overlapping events threaten to develop into a perfect storm, the like of which has not been seen since the Great Depression. To help prevent this from happening we are proposing a Green New Deal.
>
> This entails re-regulating finance and taxation plus a huge transformational programme aimed at substantially reducing the use of fossil fuels and in the process tackling the unemployment and decline in demand caused by the credit crunch. It involves policies and novel funding mechanisms that will reduce emissions contributing to climate change and allow us to cope better with the coming energy

shortages caused by peak oil. ... The Green New Deal that we are proposing consists of two main strands. First, it outlines a structural transformation of the regulation of national and international financial systems, and major changes to taxation systems. And, second, it calls for a sustained programme to invest in and deploy energy conservation and renewable energies, coupled with effective demand management.[4]

It is interesting to note that the concept of *green growth* is increasingly promoted by the political parties. We are seeing proposals for huge investment in green technologies. In particular, since the arrival of COVID-19, governments across the world have suddenly discovered that they can raise the finances necessary to respond to a major crisis.

Shifting paradigms

One of the essential steps in transitioning to a sustainable economy will be a paradigm shift in the way that people view the links between politics and the financial system. If they believe that the current system serves their best interests, then they will continue to support it. If they believe that it is causing them to suffer job insecurity, declining social services, unsafe communities, social inequality and threatens human civilization due destruction of the environment, then they will want to change it.

One of the interesting features of the 2020 US election was the emphasis that Joe Biden placed on the environment, with many of his ideas reflecting the principles of the Green New Deal. Biden obviously gets it. His election platform included commitments to spend $1.7 trillion to position the US to be a net zero economy. As a result, he predicts ten million new jobs in green economic activity. This will be underpinned by new legislation to hold polluters accountable for the damage they cause.[5]

The election of President Biden presents an opportunity for changes in the way that the American public perceive climate change, but changing paradigms is difficult. To challenge existing paradigms, it is necessary not only to highlight the dangers if we continue on the current trajectory but also to offer a positive view of a future green economy that will meet our aspirations for a better life. At present, the messages on the potential climate catastrophe are poorly understood and there is little understanding of what a future vision for a positive society might look like.

With luck, Biden's legacy will be not only that he manages to negotiate the necessary bills through the American legislative process but that he builds understanding within the American electorate of the threat from climate change, while at the same time presenting a vision for a better future. If he achieves this, it will set the stage for whoever succeeds him to also demonstrate that they are committed to a green and prosperous future.

The Green New Deal: key principles

In her book, *The Case for the Green New Deal*, Ann Pettifor identifies a number of principles that underpin the Green New Deal.

Principle 1: A steady state economy

The global economy should meet the needs of society by operating within nine ecological boundaries as measured by:

- Stratospheric ozone depletion.
- Biodiversity loss and extinctions.
- Chemical pollution.
- Climate change.
- Ocean acidification.
- Freshwater consumption/the global hydrological cycle.
- Land system change.
- Nitrogen and phosphorous release.
- Atmospheric aerosol loading.[6]

In essence, economic activity should not consume natural resources faster than they can be replenished. In part, this will be achieved by adopting the principles of a circular economy, but it also makes assumptions about the volume of material goods that people consume.

Principle 2: Limited needs, not limited wants

The current paradigm that we are entitled to limitless consumption has to change. Individuals and society as a whole need to recognize that the resources of the planet are finite. There is both a moral dimension as well as an ecological dimension to consumerism. The Green New Deal identifies *needs* such as food, housing, health, economic security and other core human rights. These are distinguished from *wants* and there is a presumption that standards of *sufficiency* will guide consumer behaviour rather than consumption without conscience.

Principle 3: Self-sufficiency

The concept of self-sufficiency is introduced in order to address issues of power, exploitation and globalization. For example, colonization was driven by opportunities to exploit the resources in other parts of the world. Similarly, globalization has enabled powerful corporations to strengthen their market influence. The concept of self-sufficiency will need to take precedence over the law of *greatest comparative advantage* and so any shift in this direction will require a revision to many of the principles that currently guide economic activity. However, as already discussed, our current presumptions of how to operate high-growth, high-consumption market economies has brought us to this point, so it is inevitable that many economic principles need to be challenged.

Principle 4: A mixed market economy

National governments face an unprecedented challenge in managing a social and economic transition from high consumption, globalized industrialized economies based on fossil fuels to sustainable, low carbon societies. To quote Ann Pettifor:[7]

> Extraordinary levels of collective effort will be required if societies are to achieve transformation of their economies away from dependence on fossil fuels and the extraction of the earth's finite assets. The scale of such efforts will be comparable to that of a nation urgently embarking on the collective effort of defence in the face of the impending war.

Principle 4, a mixed market economy, recognizes that such a transition needs to be undertaken by a mixed market economy. The role of government is likely to be ensuring that the major infrastructure is in place to support such a transition. It is also likely that governments will have a role in releasing financial resources through *green banks* that fund medium- to long-term commercial projects. However, it remains essential to harness market forces to exploit the new opportunities presented by the changes.

Principle 5: A labour-intensive economy

The original *New Deal* introduced by President Roosevelt in 1933 was a response to the Great Depression and one of its primary goals was to generate employment. Similarly, the *Green New Deal* is rooted in the goal of ensuring that the process of economic transition should protect workers displaced from industries linked to fossil fuels and should also provide new job opportunities for those currently unemployed or on the margins of work. This process of restructuring the labour market is also an opportunity to rebalance what Pettifor describes as the *obscene inequalities characteristic of late-stage capitalism*. There is a case for utilizing technology to achieve high levels of productivity rather than labour-intensive methods, but the principle is that the economy should be structured to provide meaningful work, equitable reward and to deliver economic value in ways that are sustainable.

Principle 6: Monetary and fiscal coordination for a steady state economy

Funding the transition to a sustainable economy will require massive investment in new technologies and infrastructure. There will also be a cost associated with supporting those industries undergoing transition. Financial systems have the capability to fund investment, and we have seen examples of extraordinary levels of government funds being made available to finance wars and, more recently, to bail out the banks after the financial crash of 2007–2009. During the 1930s, the original New Deal funded the American economy recovery, enabling it to lift itself out of recession. Securing the necessary funds to finance the Green New Deal is not the problem; the issue is securing the necessary level of political commitment.

Principle 7: Abandon delusions of infinite expansion

As already discussed, continual economic growth based on the exploitation of finite resources and funded by a financial system dependent on credit is, in all senses of the word, unsustainable. We have also discussed the idea that growth does not equate to an increased quality of life, nor does it ensure that all those in society benefit equally. Growth does not guarantee quality of life or national well-being. The pursuit of infinite expansion is not only impossible but it is also undesirable. The following quote from Bobby Kennedy sums it up neatly: 'it measures neither our wit nor our courage, neither our wisdom nor our learning, neither our compassion nor our devotion to our country... It measures everything, in short, except that which makes life worthwhile.'[8]

This brief summary of the principles of the Green New Deal illustrate the range of social, financial and economic issues being addressed by those working on these ideas. There are some areas where the rationale needs further investigation, and there are undoubtedly areas that will be disputed by those that have different economic or philosophical views.

The current status of the Green New Deal may have gaps in the argument, but it does provide an essential baseline upon which the next level of detail can be built. It challenges neoliberal economics and highlights the failings of the current financial system. It offers a pathway to a sustainable future that is based on a desire to combine a response to the existential threat facing the planet with an opportunity to secure a stable and equitable future society.

15

Can We Make It?

Chapter summary

This chapter considers whether civilization is likely to make the transition to a sustainable society before it is too late. The scientific indicators show that things continue to move in the wrong direction, and we can observe for ourselves the growing catalogue of natural disasters, species extinctions and ever-greater destruction of the natural environment. The actions of governments need to be judged not on whether they are doing some good things but whether they will achieve the necessary outcomes in the required time-frame.

Introduction

There was a time, not long ago, when there was only scant coverage of environmental issues on television or radio, but these days it is covered daily in news bulletins, documentaries and dedicated programmes. This increased focus on climate change and our impact on the natural world is raising awareness of the threats we face. There is growing public concern, and political parties place the green agenda at the forefront of their policies. Many corporate leaders have sensed the changing social mood and increasingly understand the scale of the threat presented by climate change. There are outstanding individuals who are championing environmental innovation and leading changes within their organizations. Corporate strategies are responding to shifts in consumer expectations and anticipating the implications of new environmental regulations. We are seeing significant investment in sustainable technologies that offer the hope of a more sustainable society.

There are many positive signs and this news should be celebrated, but we should not relax with a sense of relief that everything will be all right. The harsh reality must not be ignored; the pace of change is too slow and global temperatures are likely to continue rising. A report by the UN includes the following statement within the executive summary: 'Pathways reflecting current NDCs [Nationally Determined Contributions] imply global warming of about 3°C by 2100, with warming continuing afterwards.'[1]

Increases in global temperatures of 3°C and above will almost certainly take us past the tipping point. We are not just facing greater incidence of dangerous weather, fires, floods, crop failures and all the other horrors that will follow, but the entire climate of the planet will change in ways that threaten the survival of many life forms currently on earth.

The projections are not good, but even in the unlikely event that we do manage successfully to achieve net zero by 2050, this only gives us a 50 per cent chance that we will remain within the target of 1.5°C. The reality is that many politicians are trying to balance the different priorities of the economy and the environment rather than treat the environment as *the priority*. For many political leaders, sustaining the economy takes precedence over the environment. However, as has been seen in those countries that successfully controlled COVID-19, it is necessary to manage the crisis first, only then can economic activity return to normality.

Unfortunately, the next decade will almost certainly be characterized by lots of good intentions, some genuine progress, but ultimately, too little, too late. The executive summary of the report by the UN Environment Programme, Emissions Gap Report, 2018, states that:[2]

Technically, it is still possible to bridge the gap to ensure global warming stays well below 2°C and 1.5°C, but if NDC ambitions are not increased before 2030, exceeding the 1.5°C goal can no longer be avoided. Now more than ever, unprecedented and urgent action is required by all nations. The assessment of actions by the G20 countries indicates that this is yet to happen; in fact, global CO_2 emissions increased in 2017 after three years of stagnation.

It seems almost certain that global warming will continue to rise above 2°C. While many of us have yet to experience the consequences of climate change there are some regions of the world where it is already threatening the survival of communities. In the last few years, extreme weather events have claimed thousands of lives, caused billions of dollars of damage and displaced millions of people.

The reality of global warming is starting to bite

One of the most potent examples from 2019 was the devastation caused by bush fires in Australia. In the last few months of 2019, we saw vast areas of south eastern Australia devastated. Twelve million acres were destroyed and the fires continued to burn into 2020.

Australia is just one of many countries that have suffered the devastating consequences of climate change over the last few years. Other events include:

- California, US: During 2018–2019 forest fires caused huge economic damage and destroyed communities with more than 150,000 people being displace from their homes.
- Bahamas and South East US: In 2019, hurricane Dorian caused an estimated $4.6 billion worth of damage and killed 673 people.
- Jakarta, Indonesia: In December 2019, Jakarta was hit by floods that left an estimated 30,000 people homeless.
- Argentina and Uruguay: Floods displaced 11,000 people from their homes.
- Mozambique, Zimbabwe and Malawi: Cyclone Idai killed 1,300 people.
- Bangladesh: Severe floods are estimated to have affected five million people.
- India: Extreme monsoon weather killed 1,900 people.

- Europe: 2019 saw extreme weather conditions in many parts of Europe, causing devastation in France, Italy, Spain, Greece, the UK and elsewhere across Europe.

A report in *The Guardian*, by Fiona Harvey on 27 December 2019 gave a summary of the costs of extreme weather events: 'Climate breakdown played a key role in at least 15 events in 2019 that cost more than $1 billion (£760 million) in damage, with more than half of those costing more than $10 billion each.'[3] The article included a graphic produced by Christian Aid, as shown in Figure 15.1.

Figure 15.1: The financial cost of extreme weather events

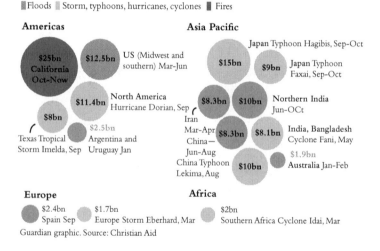

Extreme weather events across the world caused more than $100bn worth of damage in 2019

Floods ▓ Storm, typhoons, hurricanes, cyclones ▓ Fires

Americas

$25bn California Oct-Now

$12.5bn — US (Midwest and southern) Mar-Jun

$11.4bn — North America Hurricane Dorian, Sep

$8bn

$2.5bn — Argentina and Uruguay Jan

Texas Tropical Storm Imelda, Sep

Asia Pacific

Japan Typhoon Hagibis, Sep-Oct

$15bn

$9bn — Japan Typhoon Faxai, Sep-Oct

$8.3bn $10bn — Northern India Jun-OCt

Iran Mar-Apr

China — Jun-Aug

$8.3bn $8.1bn — India, Bangladesh Cyclone Fani, May

China Typhoon Lekima, Aug

$10bn

$1.9bn — Australia Jan-Feb

Europe

$2.4bn Spain Sep

$1.7bn Europe Storm Eberhard, Mar

Africa

$2bn Southern Africa Cyclone Idai, Mar

Guardian graphic. Source: Christian Aid

Source: Christian Aid, appeared in *The Guardian*. 27 December 2019.

The enormous cost of climate change

In the last few years, the impact of climate change has resulted in millions of people being displaced, thousands of people being killed and huge costs to national economies. We are continually confronted with compelling evidence that the planet is in imminent danger, yet human nature is brilliantly effective at filtering out the things that are unpleasant or frightening. There is a risk that during the next decade there will be ever more dramatic media coverage of environmental disasters, yet individually, our response will be to give a sigh of relief that it has not affected us directly – yet. If we continue like this, we risk marching towards irreversible global warming, not out of stupidity or ignorance but out of a misplaced hope that we, personally, might be all right and that *other people* will somehow manage to look after themselves.

Human survival is dependent upon a shared concern for others and we need to recognize that our own fate is intricately bound with the fate of others. All of us will be affected; if people in other parts of the world start to be displaced or killed, it has implications for the rest of us.

The process of transition is not just about reducing greenhouse gas emissions, it is also about a *just transition* to a better society. It is no longer acceptable for society to be guided by values and behaviours that encourage individuals and organizations to maximize their interests at the expense of others. The early chapters of this book talked about the need for a vision for future society. This vision will not only need to offer a positive economic vision, but it will also require a vision for a new set of values, attitudes and behaviours underpinning society.

Ideally, change will come about as a result of democratic processes managed by national and international governmental systems, but as already discussed, if the current political system fails to act quickly then it will create the conditions for alternative, disruptive forces. This must be avoided at all costs because any shift towards authoritarianism or anarchy will prevent ordered social change and obstruct international collaboration.

As public concern grows, the potential for political disruption will also grow and we are already seeing the growth of pressure groups and extreme campaigns. The challenge for the established political systems is to work with those that are agitating for more urgent climate action rather than seek to confront them. The challenge for campaigners is to work collaboratively with the established political structures and to harness the support they are building in ways that are constructive rather than destructive.

The idea for this book was first discussed not long after the Paris 2015 COP. At that time, articles and research had a prevailing sense that the situation was urgent but manageable. Much of the information suggested that we were several decades away from an irreversible tipping point. During the intervening period, the tone of the research has changed. There is a growing view that the tipping point will be reached within a matter of decades unless action is taken now.

This book has already explained that the Paris 2015 targets are inadequate to prevent runaway global warming. In addition, we have seen that most countries have a policy gap between the projected levels of emissions by 2050 and the targets set in Paris. Where governments do have policies, the targets are unlikely to achieve net zero carbon by 2050.

The UK is one of the countries setting ambitious goals, and in October 2017, the government launched The Clean Growth Strategy to achieve 80 per cent of 1990 CO_2 levels by 2050. The UK Clean Growth Strategy is, in many ways, an excellent document. It sets out a number of objectives; however, it is less clear on how they will be achieved. Aspirations are no longer sufficient and even if this approach does achieve an 80 per cent target, the remaining 20 per cent of emissions will still be causing global warming.

The three primary reasons for the lack of effective action on climate change can be summarized as:

- Belated, ineffective or indecisive political leadership.
- Resource use and allocation determined by commercial and financial criteria that fail to account for environmental costs or benefits.
- Financial and economic systems that encourage unsustainable consumption to drive economic growth.

These three issues have been discussed earlier in the book, and effective change will not happen until they are addressed. The scale and pace of change required is unprecedented in human civilization, and an effective response will require nations to prioritize the survival of human civilization above that of short-term economic interests.

The bottom line

The stark reality is that the future of human civilization is on a knife edge. The choices we make in the next few years (2020–2025) will determine whether our current way of life can be protected or whether climate change will lead to the collapse of civilization as we know it. Given that we all act to protect our own best interests, it is important that we recognize that our individual interests are best served by working collectively on shared objectives. If, instead, we believe that we are in competition with others, then we will seek personal advantage at the cost of others. This will not end well.

The challenge for the super-elite

We live in a world where a small number of powerful individuals are able to influence governments, control our financial systems, determine the way that global trade operates and, ultimately, how wealth is generated and distributed. The current economic model serves their purpose and some of them are likely to resist any changes that disrupt their power, wealth and influence. On the other hand, one of the hopeful signs is that many of those that exert great power and influence are concerned about the impending threat, not just from a financial perspective but also from a moral perspective. There is a growing movement among the top corporate leaders that they need to act.

The importance of these wealthy and powerful individuals cannot be underestimated. They, more than any other group, have the power to determine the future of humanity. They have access to the resources; they can put pressure on politicians; they can direct their organizations to become leaders and innovators in a new, green society. A report in *The Guardian* calculated that the wealth of the 26 richest people is greater than the wealth of the poorest 50 per cent of the global population.[4]

A report by Credit Suisse offers a comprehensive analysis of global wealth and how it is distributed. The extract below shows that 64 per cent of the global population own less than 2 per cent of household wealth. The 3.2 billion adults with wealth below US$10,000 account for 64 per cent of all adults, but just 1.9 per cent of global wealth.[5]

Figure 15.2: The global wealth pyramid

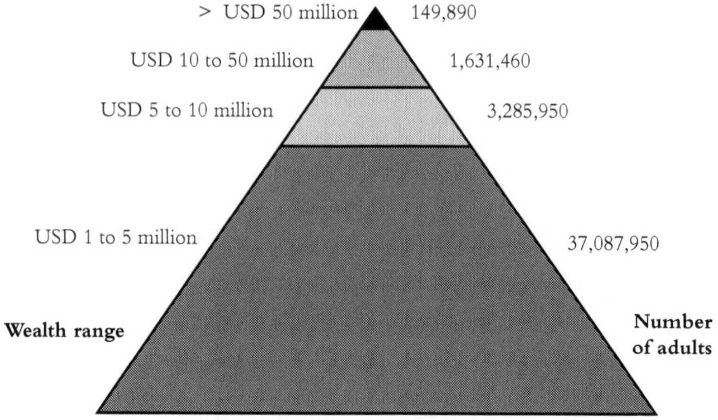

Wealth range	Number of adults
> USD 50 million	149,890
USD 10 to 50 million	1,631,460
USD 5 to 10 million	3,285,950
USD 1 to 5 million	37,087,950

Source: Global Wealth Report 2018. Credit Suisse, Research Institute

There are hopeful signs that the corporate world is increasingly concerned about the social and environmental impact of their activities. This represents an important shift in commercial priorities and values. However, the challenges are enormous, and radical corporate transition will require extraordinary courage, exceptional leadership and a new set of capabilities throughout organizations.

In conclusion

Climate change is real. The optimistic projection is that we might, with a lot of luck, just about be able to avoid runaway global warming. The pessimistic projection is that it is already too late and that we have already passed the tipping point. Even with the most optimistic projection it seems certain that the next few generations will suffer the consequences of climate chaos and the coming decades will be difficult for everyone and tragic for many. On a more positive note, the capabilities of our social and economic systems should not be underestimated. If they can be harnessed effectively, we could see advancements in technologies, economic activity and social purpose. With luck, we may be able to reverse the current trajectory.

Many of us living in advanced economies currently benefit from the wealth that has been generated by an unsustainable economic model. Ultimately, the transition to a sustainable society will require us to look inwards and reassess the things that we regard as important. Perhaps the greatest hope is that individuals are inherently good and collectively we will act to protect the planet, not just for ourselves but also for the benefit of those that come after us.

Notes

Chapter 1

1   Parts per million. Data available at: https://www.co2.earth/daily-co2
2   Global land ocean temperature index: Climate NASA. Available at: https://climate.nasa.gov/vital-signs/global-temperature
3   Cook, J. et al (2013) 'Quantifying the consensus on anthropogenic global warming in the scientific literature', *Environmental Research*, Letters 8 024024. Available at: https://iopscience.iop.org/article/10.1088/1748-9326/8/2/024024/pdf
4   Bulletin of Science, Technology and Society: Available at URL: https://journals.sagepub.com/doi/abs/10.1177/0270467619886266?journalCode=bsta&
5   The Paris Agreement. UNFCC. Article 2. Item 1.a. Available at: https://unfccc.int/sites/default/files/english_paris_agreement.pdf
6   Climate Action Tracker. Available at: https://climateactiontracker.org/global/temperatures/
7   Video clip of speech by Greta Thurnberg at the UN Climate Action Summit is available at: https://www.un.org/development/desa/youth/news/2019/09/greta-thunberg/

Chapter 2

1   Key indicators correlated to climate change. The Anthropocene website. Available at: http://www.anthropocene.info/great-acceleration.php
2   *The Telegraph*, 18 August 2011. Article by Louise Gray. Available at: https://www.telegraph.co.uk/news/earth/earthnews/8708979/Worlds-forests-absorb-almost-40-per-cent-of-man-made-CO2.html
3   CO_2 emissions from tropical forest losses. World Resources Institute. Available at: https://www.wri.org/blog/201810/numbers-value-tropical-forests-climate-change-equation
4   NASA Earth Observatory. 'The role of phytoplankton in reducing atmospheric carbon'. Available at: https://earthobservatory.nasa.gov/features/Phytoplankton/page2.php
5   Lindsay, R. (2020) 'Climate change: atmospheric carbon dioxide', *Climate. gov*, 14 August. Available at: https://www.climate.gov/news-features/understanding-climate/climate-change-atmospheric-carbon-dioxide
6   Warren, R., Price, J., Graham, E., Forstenhaeusler, N., VanDerWal, J. et al (2018) 'The projected effect on insects, vertebrates, and plants of limiting

global warming to 1.5°C rather than 2°C', *Sciencemag.org report*. Available at: https://science.sciencemag.org/content/360/6390/791#aff-1

7 *The Guardian*. 24 October 2017. 'UK is 30–40 years away from "eradication of soil fertility" warns Gove'. Available at: https://www.theguardian.com/environment/2017/oct/24/uk-30-40-years-away-eradication-soil-fertility-warns-michael-gove

8 UNCCD report published 2019. 'Land Degradation, Poverty and inequality'. Available at: https://www.unccd.int/publications/land-degradation-poverty-and-inequality

9 Sciencemag.org, 9 May 2018. Available at: https://www.sciencemag.org/news/2018/05/trump-white-house-quietly-cancels-nasa-research-verifying-greenhouse-gas-cuts

10 Chemnick, J. (2018) 'Climate change once again left out of Trump's federal budget', *Scientific American*, 11 February. Available at: https://www.scientificamerican.com/article/climate-change-once-again-left-out-of-trumps-federal-budget/

11 Milman, O. (2019) 'Climate crisis more politically polarizing than abortion for US voters, study finds', *The Guardian*, 22 May. Available at: www.theguardian.com/us-news/2019/may/21/climate-crisis-more-politically-polarizing-than-abortion-for-us-voters-study-finds

12 Willis, R. (2018) *Building the Political Mandate for Climate Change*, London: Green Alliance. Available at: https://www.rebeccawillis.co.uk/wp-content/uploads/2018/12/Building_a_political_mandate_for_climate_action.pdf

Chapter 3

1 Listings of WHO's response to COVID-19. A timeline of key notifications by WHO. Available at: https://www.who.int/news/item/29-06-2020-covidtimeline

2 Interactive data on the timeline of COVID-19 deaths from Statistica. Available at: https://www.statista.com/statistics/1092918/china-wuhan-coronavirus-2019ncov-confirmed-and-deceased-number/

3 Sample, I. (2020) 'Research finds huge impact of interventions on spread of Covid-19', *The Guardian*, 11 March. Available at: https://www.theguardian.com/world/2020/mar/11/research-finds-huge-impact-of-interventions-on-spread-of-covid-19

4 Columbia University study. Available at: https://www.voanews.com/covid-19-pandemic/delayed-us-covid-reaction-cost-lives-new-study-finds

5 First COVID-19 deaths announced in the UK. Available at: https://www.gov.uk/government/news/cmo-for-england-announces-first-death-of-patient-with-covid-19

6 Methodology for recording COVID-19 related deaths changed. Available at: https://www.gov.uk/government/news/new-uk-wide-methodology-agreed-to-record-covid-19-deaths

[7] BBC News (2020) 'China launches coronavirus "close contact detector app"', 11 February. Available at: https://www.bbc.co.uk/news/technology-51439401

[8] *The Guardian*. 18 June 2020. Available at: https://www.theguardian.com/world/2020/jun/18/uk-poised-to-abandon-coronavirus-app-in-favour-of-apple-and-google-models

[9] *The Independent*, 10 June 2020. Available at: https://www.independent.co.uk/news/uk/politics/coronavirus-track-trace-app-nhs-matt-hancock-launch-date-boris-johnson-a9558736.html

[10] Pegg, D. (2020) 'What was Exercise Cygnus and what did it find?' *The Guardian*, 7 May. Available at: https://www.theguardian.com/world/2020/may/07/what-was-exercise-cygnus-and-what-did-it-find

[11] See, for example, article in *The Guardian*. Available at: https://www.theguardian.com/business/2007/dec/18/goldmansachs.banking

[12] Mendoza, K.-A. (2012) 'Is there such a thing as ethical capitalism?' *OpenDemocracy.net*, 3 February. Available at: https://www.opendemocracy.net/en/opendemocracyuk/is-there-such-thing-as-ethical-capitalism/

[13] Eaton, G. (2020) 'The UK's national debt has surged to 100 percent – but there is no need for austerity, *The New Statesman*, 19 June. Available at: https://www.newstatesman.com/politics/economy/2020/06/uk-s-national-debt-has-surged-100-cent-there-no-need-austerity

[14] Poll of Polls. United Kingdom: National parliament voting intention. Available at: https://www.politico.eu/europe-poll-of-polls/united-kingdom/

[15] Beer, T. (2020) 'Trump disapproval rating at new high in new poll as American are embarrassed by coronavirus response', *Forbes*, August. Available at: https://www.forbes.com/sites/tommybeer/2020/08/19/trump-disapproval-rating-at-new-high-in-new-poll-as-americans-embarrassed-by-coronavirus-response/#e82fd3e2d995

Chapter 4

[1] Riversimple business principles. Available at: https://www.riversimple.com/whole-system-design/

[2] Transcript of President Obama's State of the Union Address, 2010. Available at: https://obamawhitehouse.archives.gov/the-press-office/remarks-president-state-union-address

[3] Treanor, J. (2015) 'Half of world's wealth now in hands of 1% of population – report', *The Guardian*, 13 October. Available at: https://www.theguardian.com/money/2015/oct/13/half-world-wealth-in-hands-population-inequality-report

[4] Article by Steve Denning in *Forbes*. Available at: https://www.forbes.com/sites/stevedenning/2018/05/13/france-attacks-the-worlds-dumbest-idea-maximizing-shareholder-value/?sh=7663155f46f7

[5] Harman, W. and Sahtouris, E. (1998) *Biology Revisioned*, Berkeley, CA: North Atlantic Books.

Chapter 5

[1] An example of the literature on the topic of uncertainty and future threat is captured in a paper by Dan W. Grupe and Jack B. Nitschke. 'Uncertainty and Anticipation in Anxiety'. Available at: https://www.ncbi.nlm.nih.gov/pmc/articles/PMC4276319/

Chapter 6

[1] Timperley, J. (2017) 'CCC: A plan to fill the UK's climate policy gap is "urgently" needed', *CarbonBrief*, 29 June. Available at: https://www.carbonbrief.org/ccc-plan-to-fill-uk-climate-policy-gap-urgently-needed

[2] Climate Change Committee (2017) *Meeting Carbon Budgets: Closing the Policy Gap. 2017 Report to Parliament.* Available at: https://www.theccc.org.uk/publication/2017-report-to-parliament-meeting-carbon-budgets-closing-the-policy-gap/

[3] WBGU – German Advisory Council on Global Change (2009) *World in Transition. A Social Contract for Sustainability. Flagship Report*, Berlin: WBGU. Available at: https://www.wbgu.de/fileadmin/user_upload/wbgu/publikationen/hauptgutachten/hg2011/pdf/wbgu_jg2011_en.pdf

[4] Carrington, D. (2019) 'UK has biggest fossil fuel subsidies in EU, finds commission', *The Guardian*, 23 January. Available at: https://www.theguardian.com/environment/2019/jan/23/uk-has-biggest-fossil-fuel-subsidies-in-the-eu-finds-commission

[5] Nuccitelli, D. (2018) 'America spends over $20bn per year on fossil fuel subsidies. Abolish them', *The Guardian*, 30 July. Available at: https://www.theguardian.com/environment/climate-consensus-97-per-cent/2018/jul/30/america-spends-over-20bn-per-year-on-fossil-fuel-subsidies-abolish-them

[6] Diesendorf, M. (2016) 'Dispelling the nuclear baseload myth: nothing renewables can't do better', *Energypost.eu*, 23 March. Available at: https://energypost.eu/dispelling-nuclear-baseload-myth-nothing-renewables-cant-better/

[7] Reuters article. Available at: https://www.reuters.com/article/us-climate-change-denmark-windpower-idUSKBN1Z10KE

[8] Statistical release 25 March 2021, Department for Business Energy and Industrial Strategy. Section 6. Renewables. Available at: https://assets.publishing.service.gov.uk/government/uploads/system/uploads/attachment_data/file/972790/Energy_Trends_March_2021.pdf

[9] Reuters (2018) 'China's renewable power capacity up 12 percent on year', 28 January. Available at: https://uk.reuters.com/article/us-china-renewables/chinas-2018-renewable-power-capacity-up-12-percent-on-year-idUKKCN1PM0HM

[10] BP Report, Statistical Review of World Energy 2020, referenced at Forbes.com. Available at: https://www.forbes.com/sites/rrapier/2020/06/20/bp-review-new-highs-in-global-energy-consumption-and-carbon-emissions-in-2019/?sh=4ee1f9ea66a1

[11] Rapier, R. (2021) 'Fossil fuels still supply 84 percent of world energy – and other eye openers from BP's annual review', *Forbes*, 20 June. Available at: https://www.forbes.com/sites/rrapier/2020/06/20/bp-review-new-highs-in-global-energy-consumption-and-carbon-emissions-in-2019/?sh=7335d71366a1

[12] The IPCC Assessment Report, AR5, offers projections for global temperature. Available at: https://www.ipcc.ch/report/ar5/syr/

Chapter 7

[1] Ophuls, W. (2012) 'Immoderate Greatness. CreateSpace Independent Publishing Platform'. Quotation taken from the preface.

[2] Elkington, J. (2004) 'Enter the triple bottom line', PDF. Available at: http://www.23dd.fr/images/stories/Documents/DD/Elkington-Enter-the-triple-bottom-line.pdf

[3] Education and Skills Funding Agency (2021) 'Guidance: streamlined energy and carbon report (SECR)', *Gov.uk*. Available at: https://www.gov.uk/government/publications/academy-trust-financial-management-good-practice-guides/streamlined-energy-and-carbon-reporting

[4] UN Department of Economic and Social Affairs (2020) *World Social Report: Inequality in a Rapidly Changing World – Executive summary*. Available at: https://www.un.org/development/desa/dspd/wp-content/uploads/sites/22/2020/02/World-Social-Report2020-ExecutiveSummary.pdf

[5] The European Commission (2011) 'Green accounting as the path to a sustainable future', *Greenbiz.com*, 27 April. Available at: https://www.greenbiz.com/blog/2011/04/27/green-accounting-path-sustainable-future

[6] Sir Ronald Cohen (2020). 'Impact: Reshaping Capitalism to Drive Real Change'. London: Penguin Books.

Chapter 8

[1] A more detailed explanation of these concepts is available in a book by Tony Mann (2010) *Participate for a Change: A Manual of Models & Tools for Participative Change Management*, Sutton Coldfield: RB Publishing House.

Chapter 9

[1] Dimock, M. and Wike, R. (2020) 'America is exceptional in the nature of its political divide', *Fact Tank, Pew Research Centre*, 7 May. Available at: https://www.pewresearch.org/fact-tank/2020/11/13/america-is-exceptional-in-the-nature-of-its-political-divide/

[2] Lewis, C. (2019) 'Why are taxpayers subsidising the oil and gas companies?' *The Guardian*, 30 April. Available at: https://www.theguardian.com/commentisfree/2019/apr/30/taxpayers-subsidising-oil-gas-companies-jeopardise-future

[3] Ahmed, K. (2020) '"A critical situation": Bangladesh in crisis as monsoon floods follow super-cyclone', *The Guardian*, 24 July. Available at: https://www.theguardian.com/global-development/2020/jul/24/a-critical-situation-bangladesh-in-crisis-as-monsoon-floods-follow-super-cyclone

[4] National Geographic article on hurricane Katrina, published 16 January 2019. Available at: https://www.nationalgeographic.com/environment/article/hurricane-katrina

[5] National Geographic article on Storm Sandy, published 11 February 2019. Available at: https://www.nationalgeographic.com/environment/article/hurricane-sandy

[6] National Geographic article on 2018 forest fires in California, published 13 November 2018. Available at: https://www.nationalgeographic.com/environment/article/how-california-fire-catastrophe-unfolded

[7] *The Guardian*, 24 February, 2020. Lisa Fox, Australian bush fires. Available at: https://www.theguardian.com/australia-news/2020/feb/25/unprecedented-globally-more-than-20-of-australias-forests-burnt-in-bushfires

Chapter 10

[1] *The Guardian*. 'Climate email hackers had access for more than a month'. Published 27 November 2009. Available at: https://www.theguardian.com/environment/2009/nov/27/climate-email-hackers-access-month

[2] Pettifor, A. (2020) *The Case for the Green New Deal*, New York: Verso.

Part 3

[1] Speech by Sir David Attenborough at the World Economic Forum in 2019. Available at: https://www.theguardian.com/tv-and-radio/2019/jan/21/david-attenborough-tells-davos-the-garden-of-eden-is-no-more

Chapter 11

[1] Raskin, P., Banuri, T., Gallopin, G., Gutman, P., Hammond, A., Kates, R. and Swart, R. (2002) *The Great Transition: The Promise and Lure of the Times Ahead*, Stockholm: Stockholm Environment Institute.

[2] Schumacher, E.F. (1973) *Small is Beautiful: A Study of Economics as if People Mattered*. Altrincham: Abacus.

[3] Samuel Alexandra and Rupert Read. 'This Civilisation is Finished'. Quotation from the book is available at: https://www.resilience.org/stories/2019-06-17/this-civilisation-is-finished/

[4] Northwestern University (2020) 'New technique seamlessly converts ammonia to green hydrogen', *Science Daily*, 18 November. Available at: https://www.sciencedaily.com/releases/2020/11/201118141718.htm

[5] Timperley, J. (2018) 'If the cement industry were a country, it would be the third largest emitter in the world', *Carbon Brief*, 13 September. Available at: https://www.carbonbrief.org/qa-why-cement-emissions-matter-for-climate-change

[6] Hawken, H. (2017) *Drawdown*, London: Penguin Books. The book provides a comprehensive analysis of the factors that contribute to climate change.

Chapter 12

[1] Institute for government. National commitments to achieve net zero by 2050. Available at: https://www.instituteforgovernment.org.uk/explainers/net-zero-target

[2] *The Guardian*. 'What China's plan for net-zero emissions by 2060 means for the climate'. Barbara Finamore. Published 5 October 2020. Available at: https://www.theguardian.com/commentisfree/2020/oct/05/china-plan-net-zero-emissions-2060-clean-technology

[3] van der Zee, B. (2017) 'UK is 30–40 years away from "eradication of soil fertility", warns Michael Gove', *The Guardian*, 24 October. Available at: https://www.theguardian.com/environment/2017/oct/24/uk-30-40-years-away-eradication-soil-fertility-warns-michael-gove

[4] Katwala, A. (2018) 'The spiraling environmental cost of our lithium battery addiction', *Wired.co.uk*, 5 August. Available at: https://www.wired.co.uk/article/lithium-batteries-environment-impact

Chapter 13

[1] UN FAO document, *Livestock and Landscapes*. Available at: http://www.fao.org/3/ar591e/ar591e.pdf

Chapter 14

[1] The Pope's 2015 encyclical, section VI, 54: Weak Responses. Available at: http://www.vatican.va/content/francesco/en/encyclicals/documents/papa-francesco_20150524_enciclica-laudato-si.html

[2] Society of Motor Manufacturers and Traders (2020) 'Billions invested in electric vehicle range but nearly half of all buyers still think 2035 too soon to switch', 4 September. Available at: https://www.smmt.co.uk/2020/09/billions-invested-in-electric-vehicle-range-but-nearlyhalf-of-uk-buyers-still-think-2035-too-soon-to-switch/

[3] Pettifor, A. (2020) 'Chapter 3: Global system change', *The Case for the Green New Deal*, New York: Verso.

[4] Simms, A., Pettifor, A., Lucas, C., Secrett, C., Hines, C., Leggett, J., Elliot, L., Murphy, R. and Juniper, T. (2008) *A Green New Deal: Joined-Up Policies To Solve the Triple Crunch of the Credit Crisis, Climate Change and High Oil Prices*, New Economics Foundation, 20 July. Available at: https://neweconomics.org/2008/07/green-new-deal

[5] Joe Biden presidential 2020 election campaign video. President Biden commits to a green economy. Available at: https://joebiden.com/climate-plan/

[6] Stockholm Resilience Centre, Stockholm University. Nine ecological boundaries. Available at: stockholmresilience.org

[7] Pettifor , A.(2019), *The Case for the Green New Deal*, New York: Verso.
[8] Robert F. Kennedy speech at the University of Kansas, 18 March 1968.

Chapter 15

[1] United Nations Environment Programme (2018) *Emissions Gap Report 2018*, 27 November. Available at: https://www.unep.org/resources/emissions-gap-report-2018

[2] UN Environment Programme Report: Emissions Gap Report 2018. Available at: https://wedocs.unep.org/bitstream/handle/20.500.11822/26895/EGR2018_FullReport_EN.pdf?isAllowed=y&sequence=1

[3] Harvey, F. (2019) The financial cost of climate breakdown. Available at: https://www.theguardian.com/world/2019/dec/27/climate-crisis-linked-to-atleast-15-1bn-plus-disasters-in-2019

[4] Elliot, L. (2019) 'World's richest people own as much as poorest 50%, says Oxfam', *The Guardian*, 21 January. Available at: https://www.theguardian.com/business/2019/jan/21/world-26-richest-people-own-as-much-as-poorest-50-per-cent-oxfam-report

[5] Credit Suisse, Research Institute. Global Wealth Report 2018. Available at: https://www.credit-suisse.com/about-us-news/en/articles/news-and-expertise/global-wealth-report-2018-us-and-china-in-the-lead-201810.html

Index

References to figures appear in *italic* type;
those in **bold** type refer to tables.